NEBSM SUPER SERIES
Second Edition

Managing Information

IN5

WRITING SKILLS

D1354594

Published for
The National Examining Board for Supervisory Management

by
Pergamon Open Learning
division of
Pergamon Press Ltd
Oxford · New York · Seoul · Tokyo

U.K.	Pergamon Press Ltd, Headingᴛᴏ_ OX3 0BW, England
U.S.A.	Pergamon Press Inc, 660 White Plains Road, Tarrytown, New York 10591, NY, USA
KOREA	Pergamon Press Korea, KPO Box 315, Seoul 110-603, Korea
JAPAN	Pergamon Press, 8th Floor, Matsuoka Central Building, 1-7-1 Nishi-Shinjuku, Shinjuku-ku, Tokyo 160, Japan

This unit supersedes the Super Series first edition unit 302 (first edition 1985)

Second edition 1991
Reprinted 1992

A catalogue record for this book is available from the British Library

ISBN book and cassette kit: 0-08-041607-1

The views expressed in this work are those of the authors and do not necessarily reflect those of the National Examining Board for Supervisory Management or of the publisher

Original text produced in conjunction with the Northern Regional Management Centre under an Open Tech Contract with the Manpower Services Commission.

Design and Production: Pergamon Open Learning

NEBSM Project Manager: Pam Sear

Author: Howard Senter
First Edition Author: Diana Thomas
Editor: Diana Thomas
Series Editor: Diana Thomas

Typeset by BPCC Techset Ltd, Exeter
Printed in Great Britain by BPCC Wheatons Ltd, Exeter

CONTENTS

1 Welcome to the User Guide

Hello and welcome to the NEBSM Super Series second edition (Super Series 2) flexible training programme.

It is quite likely that you are a supervisor, a team leader, an assistant manager, a foreman, a section head, a first-line or a junior manager and have people working under you. The Super Series programme is ideal for all, whatever the job title, who are on or near that first rung of the management ladder. By choosing this programme we believe that you have made exactly the right decision when it comes to meeting your own needs and those of your organization.

The purpose of this guide is to help you gain the maximum benefit both from this particular workbook and audio cassette and also from a full supervisory management training programme.

You should read the whole of this User Guide thoroughly before you start any work on the unit and use the information and advice to help plan your studies.

If you are new to the idea of studying or training by yourself or have never before worked with a tutor or trainer on an individual basis, you should pay particular attention to the section below about Open Learning and tutorial support.

If you are a trainer or tutor evaluating this material for use with prospective students or clients, we think you will also find the information given here useful as it will help you to prepare and conduct individual pre-course counselling and group briefing sessions.

2 Your Open Learning Programme

What do we mean by 'Open Learning'?

Let's start by looking at what is meant by 'Open Learning' and how it could affect the way you approach your studies.

Open Learning is a term used to describe a method of training where you, the learner, make most of the decisions about *how*, *when* and *where* you do your learning. To make this possible you need to have available material, written or prepared in a special way (such as this book and audio cassette) and then have access to Open Learning centres that have been set up and prepared to offer guidance and support as and when required.

Undertaking your self-development training by Open Learning allows you to fit in with priorities at work and at home and to build the right level of confidence and independence needed for success, even though at first it may take you a little while to establish a proper routine.

The workbook and audio cassette

Though this guide is mainly aimed at you as a first time user, it is possible that you are already familiar with the earlier editions of the Super Series. If that is the case, you should know that there are quite a few differences in the workbook and audio cassette, some of which were very successfully trialled in the last 12 units of the first edition. Apart from the more noticeable features such as changes in page layouts and more extensive use of colour and graphics, you will find activities, questions and assignments that are more closely related to work and more thought-provoking.

The amount of material on the cassette is, on average, twice the length of older editions and is considerably more integrated with the workbook. In fact, there are so many extras now that are included as standard that the average study time per unit has been increased by almost a third. You will find a useful summary of all workbook and cassette features in the charts below and on page vii.

Whether you are a first time user or not, the first step towards being a successful Open Learner is to be familiar and comfortable with the learning material. It is well worth spending a little of your initial study time scanning the workbook to see how it is structured, what the various sections and features are called and what they are designed to do.

This will save you a lot of time and frustration when you start studying as you will then be able to concentrate on the actual subject matter itself without the need to refer back to what you are supposed to be doing with each part.

At the outset you are assumed to have no prior knowledge or experience of the subject and can expect to be taken logically, step by step from start to finish of the learning programme. To help you take on new ideas and information, and to help you remember and apply them, you will come across many different and challenging self check tasks, activities, quizzes and questions which you should approach seriously and enthusiastically. These features are designed not only to make your learning easier and more interesting but to help you to apply what you are studying to your own work situation in a practical and down-to-earth way.

To help to scan the workbook and cassette properly, and to understand what you find, here is a summary of the main features:

The workbook

If you want:	Refer to:
To see which other Super Series 2 units can also help you with this topic	The Study links
An overview of every part of the workbook and how the book and audio cassette link together	The Unit map
A list of the main knowledge and skill outcomes you will gain from the unit	The Unit objectives
To check on your understanding of the subject and your progress as you work thorough each section	The Activities and Self checks
To test how much you have understood and learned of the whole unit when your studies are complete	The Quick quiz and Action checks
An assessment by a third party for work done and time spent on this unit for purposes of recognition, award or certification	The Unit assessment The Work-based assignment
To put some of the things learned from the unit into practice in your own work situation	The Action plan (where present)

If you want:	Refer to:
To start your study of the unit	The Introduction: Side one
To check your knowledge of the complete unit	The Quick quiz: Side one
To check your ability to apply what you have learned to 'real life' by listening to some situations and deciding what you should do or say	The Action checks: Side two

Managing your learning programme

When you feel you know your way around the material, and in particular appreciate the progress checking and assessment features, the next stage is to put together your own personal study plan and decide how best to study.

These two things are just as important as checking out the material; they are also useful time savers and give you the satisfaction of feeling organized and knowing exactly where you are going and what you are trying to achieve.

You have already chosen your subject (this unit) so you should now decide when you need to finish the unit and how much time you must spend to make sure you reach your target.

To help you to answer these questions, you should know that each workbook and audio cassette will probably take about *eight* to *ten* hours to complete; the variation in time allows for different reading, writing and study speeds and the length and complexity of any one subject.

Don't be concerned if it takes you longer than these average times, especially on your first unit, and always keep in mind that the objective of your training is understanding and applying the learning, not competing in a race.

Experience has shown that each unit is best completed over a two-week period with about *three* to *four* study hours spent on it in each week, and about *one* to *two* hours at each sitting. These times are about right for tackling a new subject and still keeping work and other commitments sensibly in balance.

Using these time guides you should set, and try to keep to, specific times, days, and dates for your study. You should write down what you have decided and keep it visible as a reminder. If you are studying more than one unit, probably as part of a larger training programme, then the compilation of a full, dated plan or schedule becomes even more important and might have to tie in with dates and times set by others, such as a tutor.

The next step is to decide where to study. If you are doing this training in conjunction with your company or organization this might be decided for you as most have quiet areas, training rooms, learning centres, etc., which you will be encouraged to use. If you are working at home, set aside a quiet corner where books and papers can be left and kept together with a comfortable chair and a simple writing surface. You will also need a note pad and access to cassette playing equipment.

When you are finally ready to start studying, presuming that you are feeling confident and organized after your preparations, you should follow the instructions given in the Unit Map and the Unit Objectives pages. These tell you to play the first part of Side one of the audio cassette, a couple of times is a good idea, then follow the cues back to the workbook.

You should then work through each workbook section doing all that is asked of you until you reach the final assessments. Don't forget to keep your eye on the Unit Map as you progress and try to finish each session at a sensible point in the unit, ideally at the end of a complete section or part. You should always start your next session by looking back, for at least ten to fifteen minutes, at the work you did in the previous session.

You are encouraged to retain any reports, work-based assignments or other material produced in conjunction with your work through this unit in case you wish to present these later as evidence for a competency award or accreditation of prior learning.

Help, guidance and tutorial support

The workbook and audio cassette have been designed to be as self-contained as possible, acting as your guide and tutor throughout your studies. However, there are bound to be times when you might not quite understand what the author is saying, or perhaps you don't agree with a certain point. Whatever the reason, we all need help and support from time to time and Open Learners are no exception.

Help during Open Learning study can come in many forms, providing you are prepared to seek it out and use it:

● first of all you could help yourself. Perhaps you are giving up too easily. Go back over it and try again;

● or you could ask your family or friends. Even if they don't understand the subject, the act of discussing it sometimes clarifies things in your own mind;

● then there is your company trainer or superior. If you are training as part of a company scheme, and during work time, then help and support will probably have been arranged for you already. Help and advice under these circumstances are important, especially as they can help you interpret your studies through actual and relevant company examples;

● if you are pursuing this training on your own, you could enlist expert help from a local Open Learning centre or agency. Such organizations exist in considerable numbers throughout the UK, often linked to colleges and other training establishments. The National Examining Board for Supervisory Management (NEBSM or NEBS Management), has several hundred such centres and can provide not only help and support but full assessment and accreditation facilities if you want to pursue a qualification as part of your chosen programme.

The NEBSM Super Series second edition is a selection of workbook and audio cassette packages covering a wide range of supervisory and first line management topics.

Although the individual books and cassettes are completely self-contained and cover single subject areas, each belongs to one of the four modular groups shown. These groups can help you build up your personal development programme as you can easily see which subjects are related. The groups are also important if you undertake any NEBSM national award programme.

Managing Human Resources				
HR1	Supervising at Work	HR10	Managing Time
HR2	Supervising with Authority	HR11	Hiring People
HR3	Team Leading	HR12	Interviewing
HR4	Delegation	HR13	Training Plans
HR5	Workteams	HR14	Training Sessions
HR6	Motivating People	HR15	Industrial Relations
HR7	Leading Change	HR16	Employment and the Law
HR8	Personnel in Action	HR17	Equality at Work
HR9	Performance Appraisal		

Managing Information				
IN1	Communicating	IN7	Using Statistics
IN2	Speaking Skills	IN8	Presenting Figures
IN3	Orders and Instructions	IN9	Introduction to Information Technology
IN4	Meetings		
IN5	Writing Skills	IN10	Computers and Communication Systems
IN6	Project Preparation		

Managing Financial Resources				
FR1	Accounting for Money	FR4	Pay Systems
FR2	Control via Budgets	FR5	Security
FR3	Controlling Costs		

Managing Products and Services				
PS1	Controlling Work	PS7	Solving Problems
PS2	Health and Safety	PS8	Productivity
PS3	Accident Prevention	PS9	Stock Control Systems
PS4	Ensuring Quality	PS10	Stores Control
PS5	Quality Techniques	PS11	Efficiency in the Office
PS6	Taking Decisions	PS12	Marketing

While the contents have been thoroughly updated, many Super Series 2 titles remain the same as, or very similar to the first edition units. Where, through merger, rewrite or deletion title changes have also been made, this summary should help you. If you are in any doubt please contact Pergamon Open Learning direct.

First Edition	**Second Edition**
Merged titles	
105 Organization Systems and 106 Supervising in the System	HR1 Supervising at Work
100 Needs and Rewards and 101 Enriching Work	HR6 Motivating People
502 Discipline and the Law and 508 Supervising and the Law	HR16 Employment and the Law
204 Easy Statistics and 213 Descriptive Statistics	IN7 Using Statistics
200 Looking at Figures and 202 Using Graphs	IN8 Presenting Figures
210 Computers and 303 Communication Systems	IN10 Computers and Communication Systems
402 Cost Reduction and 405 Cost Centres	FR3 Controlling Costs
203 Method Study and 208 Value Analysis	PS8 Productivity
Major title changes	
209 Quality Circles	PS4 Ensuring Quality
205 Quality Control	PS5 Quality Techniques
Deleted titles	
406 National Economy/410 Single European Market	

The NEBSM Super Series 2 Open Learning material is published by Pergamon Open Learning in conjunction with NEBS Management.

NEBS Management is the largest provider of management education, training courses and qualifications in the United Kingdom, operating through over 600 Centres. Many of these Centres offer Open Learning and can provide help to individual students.

Many thousands of students follow the Open Learning route with great success and gain NEBSM or other qualifications.

NEBSM offers qualifications and awards at three levels:

- the NEBSM Introductory Award in Supervisory Management;
- the NEBSM Certificate in Supervisory Management;
- the NEBSM Diploma in Supervisory Management.

The NEBSM Super Series 2 Open Learning material is designed for use at Introductory and Certificate levels.

The *Introductory Award* requires a minimum of 30 hours of study and provides a grounding in the theory and practice of supervisory management. An agreed programme of five NEBSM Super Series 2 units plus a one-day workshop satisfactorily completed can lead to this Award. Pre-approved topic combinations exist for general, industrial and commercial needs. Completed Super Series 2 units can count towards the full NEBSM Certificate.

The *Certificate in Supervisory Management* requires study of up to 25 NEBSM Super Series 2 units and participation in group activity or workshops. The assessment system includes work-based assignments, a case study, a project and an oral interview. The certificate is divided into four modules and each may be completed separately. A *Module Award* can be made on successful completion of each module, and when the full assessments are satisfactorily completed the Certificate is awarded. Students will need to register with a NEBSM Centre in order to enter for an award – NEBSM can advise you.

Students wishing to gain recognition of competence as defined by the Management Charter Initiative (MCI) or National Vocational Qualification (NVQ) lead bodies, will find that Open Learning material provides the necessary knowledge and skills required for this purpose.

Progression

Many successful NEBSM students use their qualifications as stepping stones to other awards, both educational and professional. Recognition is given by a number of bodies for this purpose. Further details about this and other NEBSM matters can be obtained from:

NEBSM Information Officer
The National Examining Board for Supervisory Management
76 Portland Place
London W1N 4AA

Super Series 2 units can be used to provide the necessary
underpinning knowledge, skills and understanding that are required
to prepare yourself for competence-based assessment.

Working through Super Series 2 units cannot, by itself, provide you
with everything you need to enter or be entered for competence
assessment. This must come from a combination of skill, experience
and knowledge gained both on and off the job. If you wish to pursue
an Open Learning route to a competence-based award you are
advised to check with NEBSM as to when and where this type of
assessment will be available through them, and with MCI at the
address below, as to the actual competency units that need to be
assessed as these are subject to change.

Management Charter Initiative
Russell Square House
10–12 Russell Square
London
WC1B 5BZ

You will also find many of the 44 Super Series 2 units of use in
learning programmes for other National Vocational Qualifications
(NVQs) which include elements of supervisory management. Please
check with the relevant NVQ lead body for information on units of
competence and underlying knowledge, skills and understanding.

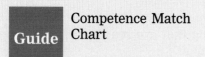

Guide Competence Match Chart

The Competence Match Chart illustrates which Super Series 2 unit provide background vital to the current Management Charter Initiativ (MCI) Supervisory sub-set Units of Competence.

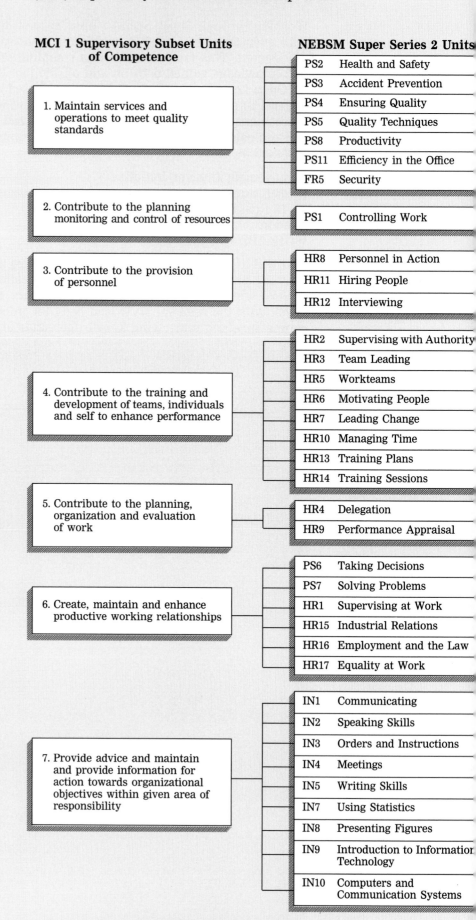

MCI 1 Supervisory Subset Units of Competence

NEBSM Super Series 2 Units

1. Maintain services and operations to meet quality standards
   - PS2 Health and Safety
   - PS3 Accident Prevention
   - PS4 Ensuring Quality
   - PS5 Quality Techniques
   - PS8 Productivity
   - PS11 Efficiency in the Office
   - FR5 Security

2. Contribute to the planning monitoring and control of resources
   - PS1 Controlling Work

3. Contribute to the provision of personnel
   - HR8 Personnel in Action
   - HR11 Hiring People
   - HR12 Interviewing

4. Contribute to the training and development of teams, individuals and self to enhance performance
   - HR2 Supervising with Authority
   - HR3 Team Leading
   - HR5 Workteams
   - HR6 Motivating People
   - HR7 Leading Change
   - HR10 Managing Time
   - HR13 Training Plans
   - HR14 Training Sessions

5. Contribute to the planning, organization and evaluation of work
   - HR4 Delegation
   - HR9 Performance Appraisal

6. Create, maintain and enhance productive working relationships
   - PS6 Taking Decisions
   - PS7 Solving Problems
   - HR1 Supervising at Work
   - HR15 Industrial Relations
   - HR16 Employment and the Law
   - HR17 Equality at Work

7. Provide advice and maintain and provide information for action towards organizational objectives within given area of responsibility
   - IN1 Communicating
   - IN2 Speaking Skills
   - IN3 Orders and Instructions
   - IN4 Meetings
   - IN5 Writing Skills
   - IN7 Using Statistics
   - IN8 Presenting Figures
   - IN9 Introduction to Information Technology
   - IN10 Computers and Communication Systems

*Please note that the Super Series 2 contains eight additional units relevant to supervisory management (see page ix).

Completion of this Certificate by an authorized and qualified person indicates that you have worked through all parts of this unit and completed all assessments. If you are studying this unit as part of a certificated programme, or think you may wish to in future, then completion of this Certificate is particularly important as it may be used for exemptions, credit accumulation or Accreditation of Prior Learning (APL). Full details can be obtained from NEBSM.

NEBSM SUPER SERIES Second Edition

IN5

Writing Skills

. . . .

has satisfactorily completed this unit.

Name of Signatory. . . . .

Position. . . . .

Signature. . . . .

Date . . . .

Official Stamp

Pergamon Open Learning and NEBS Management are always happy to hear of your experiences of using the Super Series to help improve supervisory and managerial effectiveness. This will assist us with continuous product improvement, and novel approaches and success stories may be included in promotional information to illustrate to others what can be done.

Guide

1 NEBSM Super Series 2 study links

Here are the Super Series 2 units which link with *Writing Skills*.
You may find this useful when you are putting together your study
programme, but you should bear in mind that:

- each Super Series 2 unit stands alone and does not depend upon
  being used in conjunction with any other unit

- Super Series 2 units can be used in any order which suits your
  learning needs.

ORDERS AND INSTRUCTIONS
This unit takes up the theme of organizing and presenting information and applies it to the task of giving verbal and written instructions.

COMMUNICATING
This unit looks at speaking, listening, writing and the way we behave in the broad context of the communication process.

PRESENTING FIGURES
This unit looks at the ways in which we present figures clearly and effectively - an important aspect of written communication.

WRITING SKILLS
How to organize your thoughts and write clearly and effectively to secure the response you want in letters, memos, reports and meeting documents.

MEETINGS
Contributing to and running successful meetings involves effective written skills.

PERFORMANCE APPRAISAL
A written performance appraisal can be difficult to action. This unit puts it in the context of preparing for, carrying out and following up on a performance appraisal interview.

SPEAKING SKILLS
The complementary skill to writing. How to talk to people in a clear, well organized and effective way, from a meeting in a corridor to making formal presentation to management.

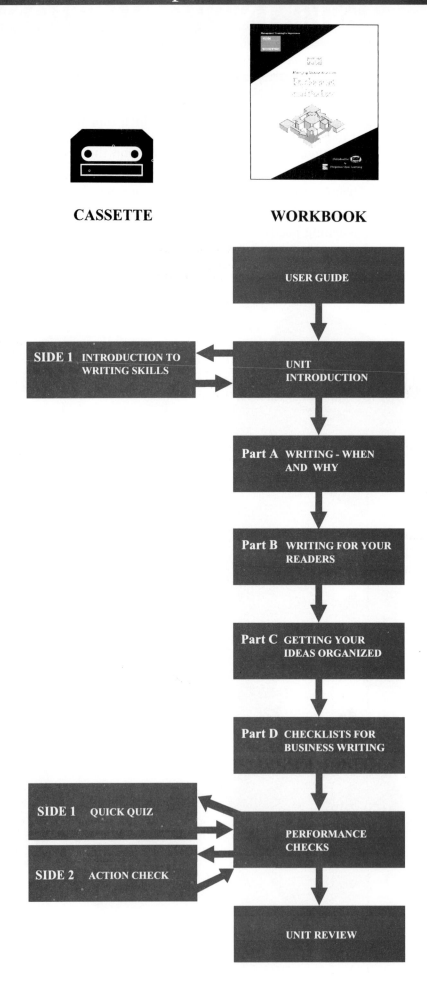

CASSETTE

WORKBOOK

```
                                    ┌─────────────────────┐
                                    │     USER GUIDE      │
                                    └──────────┬──────────┘
                                               │
                                               ▼
┌──────────────────────────┐        ┌─────────────────────┐
│ SIDE 1  INTRODUCTION TO  │◄──────►│        UNIT         │
│         WRITING SKILLS   │        │    INTRODUCTION     │
└──────────────────────────┘        └──────────┬──────────┘
                                               │
                                               ▼
                                    ┌─────────────────────┐
                                    │ Part A  WRITING - WHEN
                                    │         AND WHY     │
                                    └──────────┬──────────┘
                                               │
                                               ▼
                                    ┌─────────────────────┐
                                    │ Part B  WRITING FOR YOUR
                                    │         READERS     │
                                    └──────────┬──────────┘
                                               │
                                               ▼
                                    ┌─────────────────────┐
                                    │ Part C  GETTING YOUR
                                    │         IDEAS ORGANIZED
                                    └──────────┬──────────┘
                                               │
                                               ▼
                                    ┌─────────────────────┐
                                    │ Part D  CHECKLISTS FOR
                                    │         BUSINESS WRITING
                                    └──────────┬──────────┘
                                               │
                                               ▼
┌──────────────────────────┐        ┌─────────────────────┐
│ SIDE 1   QUICK QUIZ      │◄──────►│    PERFORMANCE      │
├──────────────────────────┤◄──────►│      CHECKS         │
│ SIDE 2   ACTION CHECK    │        └──────────┬──────────┘
└──────────────────────────┘                   │
                                               ▼
                                    ┌─────────────────────┐
                                    │    UNIT REVIEW      │
                                    └─────────────────────┘
```

All supervisors and managers have to do a certain amount of writing – letters, reports, log entries, messages, notes, faxes, training guides and so on. This does not always come easily, because most of us prefer to be ***doing*** things, rather than ***writing about them***. Indeed, for a lot of people, writing is a tedious chore, something to avoid whenever possible.

Yet there is no escaping the fact that writing is often the most appropriate means of communicating with others, and the better we can do it, the more effective we will be.

Whatever we have to write, our aim should be to put our messages across accurately, briefly and clearly – for the sake of our readers, and to achieve our own purposes.

Before you start work on this unit, listen carefully to Side one of the audio cassette, which sets the scene for our examination of *Writing Skills*.

In this unit we will:

● identify when and why we need to write;

● look at ways of developing a clear, simple style;

● examine ways of organizing what we want to say.

Objectives

When you have worked through this unit you will be ***better able to***:

● identify when and why you need to write;

● make your style of writing simple, direct and appropriate for the reader and the task;

● organize your writing so that your ideas and messages are easy to understand;

● ensure your writing achieves results.

WRITING – WHEN AND WHY?

1   Introduction

When you need to communicate with someone, you have two main options. Either you speak, or you write.

There are a few other means of communication which don't involve either of these, such as Morse Code, telepathy and sign language, but they are not practical alternatives.

Although most people find speaking easier than writing (and it was in use long before writing was invented), an enormous amount of writing goes on. About 50,000 books are published every year in Britain alone, plus hundreds of newspapers and thousands of magazines. These are all produced by professional writers – authors and journalists.

But the majority of the writing that goes on is not done by professionals at all. I am thinking of the hundreds of millions of letters, memos, reports, manuals, notices, orders, reminders, appraisals, notes and other business documents that organizations produce.

Many of these are written by people like you, and every single one is written for a purpose. So whether you like it or loathe it, writing is part of your job. And the more effectively you write, the better your job will get done.

2   Why write when you can speak?

There are obviously some situations when it is vital to speak – and when it would be stupid to write. For example, if there was a bomb warning and you had to evacuate the building, it would not be wise to inform your workteam by pinning up a notice.

Here are some more situations where speaking would be best:

- when you want to ask someone the time;
- when someone in your workteam asks for help;
- when your views are requested at a meeting;
- when you're asked for a personal opinion off the record;
- when you're showing someone how to perform a task.

Activity 1

■ Time guide 2 minutes

Think about the situations I have just described. What can you say *in general* about the situations where *speech* is better than *writing*?

_____

_____

_____

You may have put it differently, but I hope you would agree with me that there are three kinds of situation where speech is definitely the better choice:

■ when you need to communicate immediately;

■ when the person you need to reach is readily available;

■ when there is no need to put your words on record.

If you don't have to write, there is no point in doing so, because in general speech has two advantages over writing:

● it has more impact;

● it is a lot quicker.

However, writing also has some important advantages of its own. I will use a few examples to show what I mean.

The first example is a statement.

Don witnessed a nasty accident in the factory. Two machine operators were hurt when a joint on a plastic extrusion machine blew open and molten plastic was sprayed all over their hands. As soon as the ambulance had taken them away, Don's Section Manager called him into his office and asked him what he had seen. When Don had finished he said 'Right, Don. Nasty business. I think you'd better get that down in writing.'

Activity 2

■ Time guide 2 minutes

What were the advantages of having Don's statement in writing? Make a note of *two* advantages.

_____

_____

_____

Evidence will be needed because there might well be a formal investigation by the Health and Safety Executive; at the very least, the two injured workers will probably want to claim compensation, and this may go to a Tribunal. (There is also a legal requirement to enter this kind of incident in the Accident Book, but that is a separate matter.)

Human memory fades, and as time passes we become less and less able to recall events accurately; so it makes sense to get them down in writing at the first opportunity. Don's statement will be filed and used at a later date, and perhaps in a different place.

So we can sum up the advantages of a written statement by saying:

■ it creates a permanent record;

■ it is more likely to be accurate than anyone's memory;

■ it can cross both time and space to be used again.

Case
Study

The second example is a discussion paper.

Manjit had been reporting problems with a particular supplier since the beginning of the year. The purchasing committee was due to meet in a fortnight's time, and Manjit was asked to submit a full report about the problems that had occurred, giving precise details of dates, materials involved and any correspondence that had taken place. 'It needs to be completely accurate, so check your facts carefully', she was told. 'Your report will be the basis for deciding whether or not we go on using them.'

Activity 3

■ Time guide 3 minutes

What were the advantages of having Manjit put her information in writing? Make a note of *two* advantages.

_____

_____

_____

A sloppy committee would just have asked Manjit to come along and tell them about the problems. However, this is an important business matter, and it is not sensible to rely on a verbal account alone: it is bound to be incomplete, lacking in hard facts and probably somewhat biased. Far better to ask for a written report, to give Manjit time to dig up facts, dates and copies of letters, and to send copies of the report to committee members in advance of the meeting.

They can then think about it beforehand, and prepare their questions and comments. Then Manjit can be invited to attend the meeting, to answer these questions and add her own views. This is businesslike, fair and efficient.

So the advantages of having a written report in advance are:

■ it should provide a complete and detailed record of the facts;

■ it should be reliable and credible, because there is time to prepare it properly;

■ it can cross time and space to form the basis of a later discussion.

The third example is a re-call.

Case
Study

Clinton Rollers Ltd had been warned that one of their models contained a faulty component which was potentially dangerous. Although the danger was minimal, they decided to advise all their 500 customers to have machines with serial numbers CR 34900 upwards checked by their local distributor. The Customer Service department was told to send out letters explaining this within the week.

Activity 4

■ Time guide 3 minutes

What were the advantages of writing a letter rather than telephoning the customers? Make a note of *two* advantages.

_____

_____

_____

Trying to speak to all 500 customers by telephone presents a number of problems:

■ it takes a long time and a lot of expense;

■ it is difficult to be sure that they have all been given the message in a consistent way;

■ it is difficult to be sure that the message has got through accurately.

Thus on the phone a particular customer might say, 'Well, it doesn't seem that serious. I'll leave it till the end of the season.' If the person calling from Clinton's replied, 'OK – as long as you know,' and that customer later had an accident, Clinton's could find themselves in legal trouble for negligence.

So we could sum up the advantages of writing in this case by saying:

■ it is more efficient when the same message has to be sent quickly to many different people;

■ there should be less risk of a written warning being misunderstood

■ there is a permanent record of the fact that the warning has been given.

The fourth example is a procedural manual.

Watkinson's decided to put together a procedural manual which would describe the complex and varied work of the Inspection Department in detail. In future, employees joining the department would study the manual as well as getting direct instruction from the three supervisors, as before. The supervisors compiled the Manual, assisted by a training officer: when it was completed it came to a massive 180 pages.

Activity 5

■ Time guide 3 minutes

What would be the advantages of creating a written procedural manual rather than just relying on verbal instructions?

_____

_____

_____

No doubt the three supervisors all had a great deal of knowledge, but each one would have slightly different ideas and would put them in a slightly different way to his or her own trainees. This could lead to quality standards being inconsistent and different inspectors applying different procedures. With so many varied and complex tasks involved, there would probably be a good deal of uncertainty and confusion about a whole number of issues.

Having it all set out formally in a manual has several advantages:

- it provides a complete reliable and authoritative guide;

- it saves people having to commit every detail to memory;

- no-one has any excuse for not following the required procedures.

The fifth example is a quick reference card.

Case Study

In Marie's section of a large mail-order firm, labour turnover was high, and a lot of Marie's time was taken up with giving newly recruited telephone clerks basic training in the correct procedures. These took time to sink in, and the clerks frequently made mistakes, or got stuck, and had to call on Marie to help.

Marie decided to deal with this by listing the main points of each task on sheets of card, and giving a set to each clerk after the initial training session. She told them to refer to the cards when they weren't sure what to do, and only to come back to her if there was a major problem. It took her several hours to work out what the key points should be, and how to put them, but she felt the effort was worth it.

Activity 6

- Time guide 3 minutes

What would be the advantages of using a 'quick reference card' rather than telling staff what to do? Make a note of *two* advantages.

_____

_____

_____

Relying on verbal instructions only was resulting in a great deal of lost time for Marie and her clerks. Having a short summary of what to do meant that inexperienced clerks made fewer mistakes and wasted less of Marie's time.

So the advantages of writing in this example are:

- it saves time and money;

- it helps new recruits learn the job more quickly;

- it ensures consistency, because everyone has the same instructions.

The last example is the minutes of a meeting.

When Steve received the minutes of the monthly Management Meeting, he saw he was reported as saying 'that there was no question of anyone from his team being sent on the Advanced Course as they did not have the intellectual ability.' He argued with the secretary: 'That's wrong. I didn't say that!' but when he was asked whether his own notes of the meeting showed something different, he had to admit he hadn't made any. The secretary refused to change the minutes, though in the minutes of the next meeting, he did let Steve add a comment to the effect that 'he might have been hasty in his judgement.'

Activity 7

■ Time guide 3 minutes

What are the advantages of having written minutes to record what was said at a meeting? Make a note of *two* advantages.

_____

_____

_____

'Minutes' are really only notes, though they are especially accurate and rather formal notes. They are essential for keeping track of what happened in previous meetings, and for passing on views, facts and decisions to the next. In committees, many people may speak, complicated arguments may arise, and there may be disagreements. If the committee does not have an accurate record of what happened, the result will be confusion and inefficiency.

So the advantages of having written minutes are that:

■ they provide an accurate record of past discussions;

■ they can contain as much detail as required;

■ they cross space and time to inform and guide other people.

There are some other lessons from this example: it pays to make your own notes of what happens at meetings, in case a disagreement arises later. And when formal minutes are being taken it pays to think before you speak!

---

3   The advantages of writing

The main difference between speech and writing is that **speech** is temporary. Like the ripples on a pond, speech fades away without trace as soon as it has been spoken. It is fine for getting immediate action and communicating a small amount of information, but it is very **ineffective** when:

● the speaker tries to communicate too much information;

● the listeners have to remember it for too long.

Human beings generally are not very good at **listening** and **remembering**. We often mis-hear and misinterpret what we hear, and we have only a limited capacity for absorbing information through our ears. Too much, and it simply goes 'over our heads'.

We do have a large capacity for memory, but it is unreliable. We remember some things all our lives, but a lot of what we hear and read fails to stick. As time passes, memories can crumble and fade, and get hopelessly muddled.

Writing can overcome these problems – and it serves some other uses too.

**3.1
Writing as memory**

Writing is an alternative to human memory – we use books, manuals, reports and all sorts of other documents to store information for future reference. *Reference libraries* and *computer databases* are memory-substitutes on a vast scale (indeed, we often refer to 'computer memory'). But when you write a short confidential report on a member of your workteam, and someone in Personnel puts it in a file, that is basically the same process.

> Writing can provide a permanent and reliable record
> of large amounts of detailed information
> which can be used for future reference.

**3.2
Writing can cross
time and space**

Speech is best for a 'live' audience in the here-and-now. But writing can cross unlimited *distances in space* and *distances in time*.

Distance in time is really about the *permanent record* or *memory* aspect of writing. Once something is in writing, it is fairly simple to preserve it. Often, a document that you write at work will only have a limited life, and will be thrown away after a few weeks. But others will have a much longer life.

Activity 8

■ Time guide 4 minutes

Make a note of a few things you have recently written at work which will probably still exist somewhere, in someone else's files if not in yours, in a year's time:

_____

_____

_____

If your job involves a lot of 'paperwork', then scores of things you have written will probably still be on file in a year's time. I certainly keep notes of meetings, copies of letters, and even time sheets, checklists and costings – and often for many years.

This is a good reason for trying to write well: some complete stranger may be reading through your words in ten years' time!

Writing also helps us communicate across distance in space – from site to site, town to town, and even from country to country.

Of course, if the messages are urgent, simple and short, it may be better to speak across these distances – on the phone. But where the messages are less urgent, but longer and more detailed, you need to write them down.

■ Time guide 2 minutes

Make a note of some of the things which you have to communicate, in writing, over substantial distances:

_____

_____

_____

In my case, in the last few days, I have had to send several communications across the distance barrier:

■ a ten-page report on a new management training course, sent to someone 90 miles away;

■ a batch of survey questionnaires, sent to an office 30 miles away;

■ a formal letter authorizing someone to start work on a project, and spelling out what they have to do.

I *could* have passed this information on via the phone, but it would have been very foolish to do so, because there was simply too much information there for any listener to recall accurately.

If it had been *urgent*, I might have phoned with some key details, but the main document would still have to be in writing (these days, fax is a valuable alternative for urgent documents and written messages).

**3.3
Writing can be copied for consistency**

Another big advantage of written communications is that they can easily be *copied* – and copied *exactly*.

When you need to reach a *large number* of people all at the *same time* and with an *identical message*, the answer is simple – put your message in writing and copy it. This is what Clinton Rollers did in the 're-call' example a few pages back. All 500 customers got an *identical* message, which was guaranteed to contain all the relevant information.

Sending *identical* and *consistent* messages can be very important. Take contracts of employment, for instance. As you probably know, a contract can be made by word of mouth alone, and some still are. But there is a big problem with this: if you rely on speech alone, you cannot guarantee to make every contract in the same terms and with the same tone of voice.

This is bound to mean disputes, because each person will have a different recollection of what happened; there will be uncertainty, suspicion of unlawful discrimination, and all sorts of similar problems.

That is why all sensible employers use a standard written contract, with blank spaces for the individual's particular details to be written in. This ensures fairness and consistency.

**3.4
Writing as a back-up**

I do not want to give the impression that there is an 'either-or' choice between writing and speaking. As some of the examples showed, the best way to communicate may often be a combination of the two.

■ Time guide 5 minutes

Suppose you have just held a briefing session to explain to your workteam a proposal to introduce flexible working hours. At the end of the session you hand each of them a sheet of paper listing the main points of the proposal:

> Flexible working hours
>
> 1. In any four-week period you should work an average of 140 hours.
>
> 2. Daily hours can be worked between 8 a.m. and 6 p.m.
>
> 3. Up to ten hours credit or debit can be carried forward to the next four-week period.
>
> 4. Core time (11 a.m. to 3 p.m.) should be worked daily unless you are taking holiday or credit hours carried forward.
>
> 5. Hours to be worked daily should normally be arranged one week in advance, in co-operation with your supervisor and workteam.

What would you say are the benefits of giving the workteam this list, and letting them take it away with them afterwards?

_____

_____

_____

_____

I think the main benefit is simply **putting it on the record**. People aren't good listeners, and memories are unreliable. It is common for a group of people to come away from a verbal briefing with entirely different ideas about what was said and what was meant. Later, when they start to discuss the briefing among themselves, the 'story' will inevitably get even more muddled and inaccurate.

Giving them a written document will prevent confusion, because it ensures that **everyone gets the same information**.

Of course, the list is only a brief summary of the issues, and does not answer all the questions that will occur to members of the workteam. Indeed, it probably raises some questions, like the following.

● 'How do holidays fit into this?'

● 'What exactly is 'core time'?'

● 'Do lunch breaks come out of core time, or are they separate?'

That is only to be expected, because this document is not intended to give all the details and answer all the questions. A special handbook will eventually be needed to cover all that. But as an introduction to such an important and complicated change in working arrangements, it is fine.

Certainly, it will give rise to many questions, but at least everyone concerned has a written basis for that discussion, which will help keep it on the rails.

**3.5
Writing to pass
on a message**

There is a party game called 'ghosts', where the first person whisper a message to the next, who whispers it to the next, and so on. The point of the game is to see how mangled the message can get by the time it reaches the end of the chain.

This is how 'Send reinforcements, we're going to advance' ends up as 'Send three and fourpence, we're going to a dance' – and exactly the same thing can happen in reality when someone takes a verbal message for you and verbally passes it on in a mangled or incomplete form. This can cause a lot of damage, nuisance and expense, as this example shows.

Activity 11

■ Time guide 5 minutes

Alan happens to be in the office alone, at 12.45 (midday). The telephone rings. It's Dublin Bay Printers Ltd, wanting to speak to Brendan about a delivery of printing chemicals which should have turned up three days ago. They can't afford to wait more than another 24 hours. If delivery can't be guaranteed in that time, they'll cancel the order.

Alan goes to lunch at 1 pm and asks the typist in the next office to keep an eye open for Brendan and tell him to phone the printers. When Brendan gets back at 1.30 pm, she tells him a customer was ringing from Ireland about an order.

He is a busy man, with a lot of urgent jobs to do, and the message doesn't sound all that important.

Next morning an angry fax arrives cancelling the order and demanding to know why no-one has phoned back.

What should Alan have done to make sure that Brendan dealt with the problem? At least *three* things are involved.

_____

_____

_____

_____

If Alan took responsibility for answering the phone, he should also have taken responsibility for ensuring that the message got through to Brendan – and that Brendan understood it.

He couldn't relay the message directly to Brendan, who wasn't there. But he could easily have written it.

In fact, he should have made a written note *while the printers were talking to him*. Then when they rang off, he should have:

■ re-written it neatly and checked that all the details were included;

■ marked it 'URGENT';

■ put it where Brendan was bound to see it;

■ checked later to see that he had done so.

That is no doubt what you would like your colleagues to do for you – so make sure you do it for them! Here is another example to underline this point.

Activity 12

■ Time guide 5 minutes

Suppose that a particular vessel in a production area has been overheating slightly during the nightshift. The nightshift foreman has tested the temperature every hour. At the end of his shift it is running at 10° above normal, which isn't yet critical, but the temperature has been rising throughout the eight-hour period.

He could have a word with the foreman on the dayshift: 'Keep an eye on Vessel C. It's overheating by about ten per cent'.

Or he could put a report in the shift log to tell the dayshift:

■ when he had tested the vessel;

■ what his findings were;

■ that they should carry on testing at frequent intervals.

What do you think the advantages of a written report in the log would be?

_____

_____

_____

_____

The main advantage is that the nightshift foreman can make sure that **all** the information he wants to pass on is clearly written down in black and white. The dayshift foreman can then continue taking the temperature, and can use his own judgement about what action to take.

Also, if he decides to call in Maintenance, they will have the benefit of a full report of everything that has happened during **both** shifts.

There is an additional advantage: the nightshift foreman can 'cover his back' by putting all this in the log: then if something goes badly wrong during the dayshift, no-one can blame him!

Unfortunately, writing up the log is only really useful *if* the dayshift foreman is going to read it in time – and that is a big if!

I think that if it was me, I would want to make doubly sure that the message got through:

● by speaking to the dayshift foreman personally to make sure he realizes that there is a problem;

● *as well as* writing the full details in the log for the record.

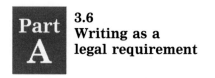

Finally, there are some situations where we need to put something i[n] writing:

■ because the law specifically requires it;

■ in order to protect ourselves if the law does get involved.

Activity 13

■ Time guide 4 minutes

What sorts of things are you required *by law* to put in writing, as part of your responsibilities at work?

_____

_____

_____

_____

Obviously this will vary a great deal, but depending on what job you do, and how wide your responsibilities are, you might have to write:

■ entries in the accident book;

■ statutory warning notices;

■ statutory certificates and authorizations;

■ statements required by police or courts;

■ appeals to Tribunals;

■ various legal documents, if you work in banking, finance or some[.] aspect of the law.

There are also several situations where employees are entitled by la[w] to have something in writing (even if it isn't you personally who has to provide it) including:

■ a written statement of terms and conditions of employment;

■ a statement of the employer's health and safety policy;

■ notification of changes in contractual terms;

■ an explanation of deductions from pay.

But the biggest area where the law needs to be considered is all those situations where you are not forced to put something in writing, but it is a good idea to do so for your own protection.

This includes any action you take which may affect someone's legal rights (job offers, disciplinary action and dismissal in particular); and anything where you may one day need to be able to **prove** what you did and what you said. So:

- if you refuse an instruction (or someone refuses an instruction from you), make a note of the time, the circumstances and what precisely happened;

- if you reply to a complaint from outside the organization, put it in writing and keep a copy;

- if you write any document with legal implications, keep a copy;

- if an incident occurs, note the details down.

4   Conclusions

It is not my intention to make you spend all your time on paperwork, or to make you paranoid about recording every little thing that happens. No doubt the majority of the time you will continue to communicate via speech.

But I hope you can see now that there are quite a lot of situations where:

- either you should write rather than speak;

- or you should speak, but back it up in writing.

It is simply a matter of using your common sense. Next time you are wondering how to get your message through most effectively, just pause for a moment and ask yourself:

'Would it be better to put this in writing?'

'Should I use writing to back up my words?'

And whenever something happens which is out of the ordinary, ask yourself:

'Would it be a good idea to make a note of that?'

Finally, writing always takes a fair bit longer than saying something out loud, but just ask yourself:

'Will I save a lot more time and trouble later, if I take the time and trouble to put it in writing now?'

■ Time guide 12 minutes

Decide whether the following statements are TRUE or FALSE.

1. When a member of your team wants advice about a work problem, it is better to put your response in writing. TRUE/FALSE

2. Many written communications are recorded permanently. TRUE/FALSE

3. When you are writing, you usually have more time to prepare and check your facts. TRUE/FALSE

4. In everyday matters, speech generally has more impact than writing. TRUE/FALSE

5. The main problem with listening to someone talking is that it is boring. TRUE/FALSE

6. Often it is advisable to use both speech and writing to ensure a communication is effective. TRUE/FALSE

Complete the following statements with a suitable word or group of words.

7. Writing is the best choice if you need to put your words on
   _____ .

8. One advantage of writing is that your communication can cross _____ and _____ .

9. Another advantage is that by copying a document to several people you can ensure they receive a _____ message.

10. The best way to communicate large amounts of information is through _____ .

11. Some things have to be in writing because this is a _____ requirement.

Answer the following questions.

12. Which came first, speaking or writing? _____

13. What is the purpose of taking minutes at a meeting?
    _____

14. What do we mean by saying written communications can cross distances in time?
    _____

15. Our memories are not very reliable. How do we store large amounts of information for later reference? Give *two* answers.
    _____
    _____

16. How does writing help you tell 'a consistent story'?
    _____

18

Response check 1

1. FALSE: this will usually be a direct spoken request; the quickest and most effective way to answer it is by speaking.

2. TRUE.

3. TRUE: sometimes you have enough time when you are going to speak on some formal occasion, but most speaking takes place in the here and now.

4. TRUE.

5. FALSE: it doesn't have to be boring. The main problem is the difficulty of concentrating, and then of remembering and recalling what was said.

6. TRUE: especially where the things which are said need to be recalled, or discussed later.

7. Writing is the best choice if you need to put your words on RECORD.

8. One advantage of writing is that your communication can cross SPACE and TIME.

9. Another advantage is that by copying a document to several people you can ensure they receive a CONSISTENT message.

10. The best way to communicate large amounts of information is through WRITING.

11. Some things have to be in writing because this is a LEGAL requirement.

12. Speaking came first (writing is a very recent skill in human terms).

13. Minutes are taken at meetings to ensure that there is an accurate record of what was said and decided.

14. 'Crossing distances in time' means putting things in writing so that they can be read by someone else later – often much later (Shakespeare's writings have crossed 400 years to reach us).

15. We store large amounts of information in computer databases, in libraries, and of course in filing systems.

16. Writing helps you tell 'a consistent story' because any written document can be copied, or repeated, exactly. Thus everyone to whom it is given will get exactly the same information.

- Writing is preferable to speaking when:
  - the communication needs to cross distances in space and time;
  - it needs to be put on record;
  - the record needs to be accurate;
  - it contains large amounts of information;
  - a back-up to spoken messages is needed;
  - a reliable basis for later discussion is needed;
  - a consistent message needs to be sent to several people.
- Some things are required by law to be in writing.
- Messages passed from person to person in speech are unreliable: write them down.
- When you have the choice of whether to speak, to write, or both, you should ask yourself the following.
  - Would it be better to put this in writing?
  - Should I use writing to back up what I have said?
  - Would it be a good idea to make a note of that?
  - Will I save a lot of time and trouble later, if I take the time and trouble to put this in writing now?

WRITING FOR YOUR READERS

1 Introduction

Sometimes we write for ourselves alone. Diaries, private notes and so on may never be read by anyone else, so it doesn't matter if no-one else can make head or tail of them. Such private writing may not be 'communication' in the usual sense at all, and it doesn't necessarily matter if we:

● use unusual words;

● use special abbreviations;

● put things in the wrong order;

● spell words wrongly;

● scribble, smudge and cross things out.

We can usually decipher our own scribbles. But when what we are writing is for other people to read, it is a very different matter. Now we are trying to communicate, and for a purpose. If they can't read what we write, or can't be sure of what we mean, then we may not achieve the result we want.

So how can we make our written communications work?

Obviously, the first step is to make sure our writing is easy to read and understand – and I don't just mean our handwriting!

2 Accurate, brief and clear

Accuracy, brevity and clarity are the three 'watchwords' for effective writing.

Accuracy means:

● getting the facts right;

● getting the grammar and spelling right.

Brevity means:

● sticking to the point;

● not using more words than you need to.

Clarity means:

● expressing yourself simply and clearly;

● using a logical structure.

Part B

I am not going to say anything about *getting the facts right*, except to say that it is up to you to **prepare** and **check** before you commit yourself to writing. Remember that writing can go on the record for a very long time: if you have made a silly factual mistake it will not be easy to get rid of it.

Grammar and spelling *are* important, though.

Activity 14

■ Time guide 2 minutes

Suppose you pin up a notice containing various errors of spelling and grammar like this.

■ The heating controls in this area must not be altared, they are pre-set by the engineers and this can damage them. The settings are done to acheive a proper heating at all times even if cold first thing.

The *meaning* of this notice is fairly clear, but what effect would the errors have?

_____

_____

A lot of people who read the notice may not realize there are errors, but you can bet your life that *someone* will. And that someone is going to think less of the writer as a result. In other words, the writer's credibility will suffer.

I am not going to explain everything that is wrong with the notice in our example, but here is an improved version of it:

■ The heating controls in this area are pre-set by the engineers to provide the correct level of heating throughout the day. Even if it seems cold first thing, *do not alter the settings*, as this can cause damage.

Extension 1 If you are not confident about avoiding common errors of this kind, you may find it helpful to look at Extension 1, which provides a brief guide to getting plurals and apostrophes right.

Correct spelling means learning words as you go along. No-one can claim to spell everything perfectly, because there are so many long and complicated words in the language. But it is very embarrassing to have your spelling corrected, and it is well worth trying to improve your spelling skills.

Activity 15

■ Time guide 6 minutes

You will need a dictionary for this activity, which is about checking your spelling. Tick the words which are correct, and write down the correct spelling of those which are wrong:

Tabulation		Bussiness	
Committee		Arguement	
Fulfill		Queue	
Necessary		Solusion	
Preparation		Corparation	
Perceive		Defendent	
Coranory		Discipline	
Instalment		Greavance	
Segment		Promise	
Independent		Equipped	

I hope you found that dictionary activity useful – obviously I don't need to give you the correct answers. It's a good idea to keep a dictionary handy whenever you have to write something. It only takes a few moments to check how to spell a word you are unsure about, and guessing wrongly can cause a lot of embarrassment! There are a number of good-sized pocket dictionaries on the market. Why not invest in one?

Grammar is a less clear-cut issue than spelling: it means the rules on how we should put our words together. This is an example of **bad grammar**:

'Where's them memos what I wrote?'

Although some people would indeed say something like that, most listeners would agree that it was incorrect grammar. And as with spelling, it becomes a much worse mistake when it is written down. The correct way to put it would be:

'Where are the memos that I wrote?'

Correct grammar is just as important as correct spelling, but it is much too big a subject for us to deal with here.

3   Plain words

Your aim when writing should be accuracy, brevity, clarity.
In practice, brevity and clarity are much the same thing: if it is brief, there is a much better chance of it being clear as well.

How brief you can make your writing depends firstly on:

> not saying more than you have to;
> using simple and straightforward language.

Here is an example of someone who seems incapable of doing either of these things:

Memo: To Tom Robinson, Production
From: Belinda Wasserman, Customer Services

Subject: Recent developments
You asked me to comment on the problems we have been experiencing recently with regard to maintaining adequate inventory for meeting agreed performance criteria for meeting customer orders for made up fabrics for the mail-order market.

Our position is already well known. There have been extreme difficulties in the recent period and this has had negative effects particularly in terms of customer complaints. These are up by a considerable margin of late.

Regarding quality we have not become aware of any substantial variation from the normal picture.

Finally, packaging standards appear to be experiencing some degree of deterioration as more has come back as damaged in the post.

Fabric-based motor accessories do not appear to present a problem as at this moment in time.

There are all sorts of things wrong with the way this memo is written, but the worst is the words and phrases Belinda uses.

In the English language there are many different ways of saying things, and there are even long and short words for a lot of things. For example:

Long	Short
Variation	Change
Deterioration	Worsening
Accessories	Parts, fittings
Maintaining	Keeping up

Clearly, if you can use shorter words which have the same meaning, you are likely to make your writing easier to understand.

Activity 16

Part
B

■ Time guide 8 minutes

Write down *one* or *two* short words which could replace the long ones in the list below. I have done the first two for you.

Long	Short	Long	Short
Advantageous	Useful	Disadvantage	
Unprecedented	New	Ascertain	
Commencement		Deficiency	
Consequently		Excessive	
Facilitate		Subsequently	
Terminate		Utilization	
Expenditure		Inventory	
Relationship		Fundamental	
Furthermore		Application	
Comprehension		Illustrate	

Which words you would use to replace these long ones depends to some extent on the context, but the ones which occurred to me are:

Long	Short	Long	Short
Advantageous	Useful	Disadvantage	Drawback
Unprecedented	New	Ascertain	Find out
Commencement	Start	Deficiency	Lack
Consequently	So	Excessive	Too much
Facilitate	Allow	Subsequently	Later
Terminate	End	Utilization	Use
Expenditure	Spending	Inventory	Stock
Relationship	Link	Fundamental	Basic
Furthermore	Also	Application	Use
Comprehension	Grasp	Illustrate	Show

Thus instead of:

'Subsequently we comprehended the fundamental disadvantages of excessive expenditure on inventory.'

we can say:

'Later we grasped the basic drawbacks of spending too much on stocks.'

The problem is not just with individual words, but with whole phrases.

Activity 17

■ Time guide 3 minutes

Suppose you received the following letter:

Dear Sir

With reference to your recent letter, we are now in a position to advise you that your order has been expedited and you should obtain receipt of the outstanding items, namely 21 OHS baffles, by 31st January latest.

Assuring you of our best attention at all times,

Yours faithfully

Jot down what you think about the *way* the letter is written.

_____

_____

_____

What impression do you form of the writer from reading the letter?

_____

_____

_____

(Don't bother about the possible inefficiency which led to the letter being necessary in the first place.)

Well, I think the first thing that strikes one is the unnatural and pompous language in which the letter is written: 'We are now in a position to advise you' and 'you should obtain receipt' are just two examples of what I mean – you may have picked out more.

We *understand* what the writer is saying but he could have said it far more simply. For example 'you should receive', or 'the order should arrive' would be better than 'you should obtain receipt'. And 'we are now in a position to advise you', could probably have been left out altogether if the sentence had been changed a little.

But worse than this, the writer uses one word, 'expedite', which quite possibly the reader wouldn't understand. In fact, it means 'hurried up', nothing more, but you suspect that the writer is using it to sound important and official.

Trying to make ourselves sound important is an understandable human weakness but it doesn't usually cut much ice! A letter like this is more likely to annoy or amuse the reader than impress him.

Finally, the writer uses some old-fashioned flowery phrases which once used to be very common in commercial writing, but which have now largely been abandoned. I mean 'With reference to' and 'Assuring you of our best attention at all times.'

Beginning something with 'with reference to' tends to involve you in writing a very cumbersome sentence. It's simpler and sounds better to deal with what you are referring to in a separate sentence like this: 'Thank you for your recent letter. I have followed up your order . . .'. And 'Assuring you of our best attention at all times', although it sounds friendly enough, could well be replaced by something simpler like: 'We apologize for the delay', in the example we've been looking at.

So this letter would be much better if the writer:

● *made the point as briefly as possible*;

● *used common words rather than difficult words*;

● *used simple and natural expressions rather than flowery ones to open and close the letter.*

And if he had done these things the letter might read something like this:

Dear Sir

Thank you for your recent letter.

I have followed up your order for 21 OHS baffles which should reach you before 31st January.

I apologize for the delay.

Yours faithfully

Activity 18

■ Time guide 5 minutes

Here's another example of a pompous, wordy piece of writing – this time a memo. Rewrite the memo on the memo form provided, making it as simple and to the point as you feel it should be.

Memorandum	
From: Office Supervisor	To: All Office Staff
Subject: Training Sessions	Date: 10 Jan.

It has been decided by the Training Officer to hold one-day training sessions in word processing and the use of the spreadsheet package for all staff wishing to avail themselves of this facility.

I am instructed to ask you to notify me by Friday 18 January of your intention with regard to these courses and to indicate your preferred dates.

The courses will be held on 25/26 February (Word processing)
27/28 February (Spreadsheet)

M.C.T.

Memorandum	
From: Office Supervisor	To: All Office Staff
Subject: Training Sessions	Date: 10 Jan.

M.C.T.

Everybody is likely to have written something slightly different for this but here is my version for you to compare with yours. You'll see that it's much shorter than the original and has got rid of the more long-winded expression – but it's quite possible that yours is an improvement on mine.

Memorandum	
From: Office Supervisor	To: All Office Staff
Subject: Training Sessions	Date: 10 Jan.

The Training Officer will be holding one-day courses on word processing and the use of the spreadsheet package on the following dates:

> 25/26 February (Word processing)
> 27/28 February (Spreadsheet)

All staff are invited so, if you would like to attend, would you please let me know which course you are interested in and the date you prefer by Friday 18 January.

M.C.T.

So, I hope we can agree we can improve the standard of what we write straight away if we choose the simplest way of saying what we want. And this always means finding **our own** way of saying something rather than using somebody else's overworked expression.

The problem is that long-winded ways of saying things can become very common and, because we hear and read them so often, they are often the first expressions which come to mind.

Here are a few examples of what I mean with a simpler alternative shown beneath them.

- with regard to;

  about;
- a large proportion of;

  many;
- at an early date;

  soon;
- at the present moment in time;

  currently/now;
- in consequence of;

  because of/owing to;
- due to the fact that;

  because/owing to.

If we try putting these expressions in a sentence we can see that the simpler alternative puts the idea across more effectively and saves time and energy for the writer and the reader.

● A large proportion of those attending the course had no previous management experience.

Many of those attending the course had no previous management experience.

● It was agreed that the group should meet at an early date.

It was agreed that the group should meet again soon.

● We are out of stock at the present moment in time.

We are currently out of stock.

● In consequence of the Secretary's resignation, the meeting was postponed for a week.

Because of the Secretary's resignation, the meeting was postponed for a week.

Incidentally, writing things as simply as possible tends to show up ideas and decisions for what they really are.

Let's look at one of these examples again.

'It was agreed that the group should meet again soon.'

Anybody reading that might reasonably think that the group should have done better and fixed a date for their next meeting. Writing 'at an early date' might just be a not very successful attempt to look more efficient than they really were!

Activity 19

■ Time guide 5 minutes

Here are some more examples of sentences containing long-winded, overworked expressions which can be replaced by simpler, clearer ones. Jot down what you think would be a better word to use in each of these sentences instead of the group of words highlighted.

■ ***Despite the fact that*** deliveries of raw materials were late, the order was met on time.

_____

■ This ***in many cases*** proved to be so.

_____

■ I should like to ***draw your attention to the fact*** that I haven't been paid.

_____

■ We must ***give due consideration to*** the staff development programme.

_____

■ In ***view of the fact that*** I am retiring this year, ***I am of the opinion*** that somebody else should undertake the long-term project.

_____

■ All departments, ***with the exception of*** Data Processing, were represented.

_____

Here are my suggestions, though other words would do as well in some cases. I've written the whole sentence out each time so that you can see that using a simpler expression improves the sentence and doesn't affect the meaning in any way.

- *Although* deliveries of raw materials were late, the order was met on time.

- This *often* proved to be so.

- I should like to *point out* that I haven't been paid.

- We must *consider* the staff development programme.

- *Since* I am retiring this year, I *think* that somebody else should undertake the long-term project.

- All departments *except* Data Processing were represented.

If we were writing a checklist for 'How to Make Your Writing as Long-Winded as Possible' we could say:

- don't think for yourself, use whatever wordy expressions are current (and don't worry too much about the meaning);

- if one word will do, use six.

And we could add to that:

- make sure you say the same thing twice wherever possible.

If we look closely at some overworked expressions, we can see that all they are doing is repeating an idea which has already been expressed in a previous word. Here are some examples of what I mean:

- 'the reason why this is so is because';

- 'advance planning';

- 'my own personal opinion'.

In any sentence 'the reason is', 'why' and 'because' all convey the same idea – you don't need all three.

And, if we look at 'advance planning', planning *has* to be in advance – you certainly can't plan for what has already happened!

And, looking at 'my own personal opinion', well, whose opinion can mine be except my own? So 'my opinion' should be enough.

Extension 2 An excellent guide to accurate, brief and clear writing is *The Complete Plain Words* by E. Gowers. Although first written back in 1948 to show Civil Servants how to make their writing more readable, it is still thoroughly relevant. Chapters 5, 6, 7 and 8 are about choosing the simple, familiar and precise words.

Activity 20

- ■ Time guide 3 minutes

Here are some more sentences in which the same idea has been expressed twice. Cross out the word or group of words which you feel is unnecessary.

- ■ The subject of the Finance Director's address will be about the financial forecast for next year.

- ■ Every single opportunity will be taken.

- ■ We will continue to remain staying on course.

- ■ Every individual person must sign this.

Here are my suggestions.

- ■ The Finance Director's address will be about the financial forecast for next year./The subject of the Finance Director's address will be the financial forecast for next year.

- ■ Every opportunity will be taken.

- ■ We will continue on course./We will remain on course./We will stay on course.

- ■ Every individual must sign this./Everybody must sign this.

So, it's important to check that, when you write something, you're not just repeating something you've already said in a different way.

Earlier on we said that trying to write simply tends to show up ideas and decisions for what they really are. Conversely, if people want to disguise the truth or if they are simply not very sure of what they are saying, they tend to wrap things up in a blanket of words to put the reader off the track.

Of course, this may not always be deliberate but, as a reader and a writer, it's something against which you must be on your guard.

4   Honest and dishonest expressions

Let's look at two kinds of common dishonesty that you sometimes find in writing – this doesn't apply only to the sort of written information we come across at work; political statements are often full of very slippery pieces of writing.

Sometimes it is a matter of the choice of words – you can make Stock Control sound much more impressive by calling it Inventory Management – but sometimes it is the ideas which need careful watching.

Activity 21

■ Time guide 3 minutes

Read the following statements. They are all about the lack of storage space in a particular section of a factory. But what is the writer trying to suggest about the problem in each statement? Jot down what you feel he is trying to do.

■ As is well known, storage space in B Section has been insufficient for a number of months.

_____

_____

■ It is evident that present storage arrangements are inadequate.

_____

_____

■ It is generally agreed that the problem of the lack of proper storage in B Section must have high priority.

_____

_____

■ For obvious reasons, storage problems in B Section must be dealt with speedily.

_____

_____

He's trying to suggest that he has support from other people for the views he is expressing:

■ 'as is well known...';

■ 'it is evident that...';

■ 'it is generally agreed that...'.

Now, if he provides **evidence** of that support, we can perhaps accept his argument, but in these particular statements he's not providing any evidence at all, just **saying** that the support is there. And if a piece of writing containing comments like these arrived on your desk, then you would have to read it very critically.

Similarly, in the last statement, he is suggesting that the reasons backing up his point of view are so apparent that they don't need saying. That's something which should always be treated with great suspicion.

So one common kind of dishonest writing is:

suggesting that your argument is better supported than it really is.

The second kind of dishonesty is, I think, even worse and, in my experience, is rarely unintentional.

Let me give you an example of what I mean.

'In the past year we have made several changes in our personnel structure and streamlined our organization considerably. These improvements are now beginning to pay off and I'm sure that, in the next quarter, we shall find...'.

Did you notice that at first the writer refers to 'changes' in the personnel structure, but the next time he mentions them in the following sentence he refers to them as 'improvements'? And, as we all know, changes aren't necessarily improvements. We would need to be convinced by some evidence that changing the personnel structure had actually brought about some improvements.

Activity 22

■ Time guide 3 minutes

Here are two more instances of dishonest writing similar to the example we have just looked at.

Jot down how you think the writer is 'cheating' in each case.

■ In the Data Processing department we have the example of a section supervisor who started with the company in Marketing and, following retraining, has moved successfully into Data Processing. I see this trend continuing throughout the company.

_____

_____

_____

■ The manager's opinion is that the fall of the pound against the dollar should increase our sales in the short term. This fact encourages me to think that . . . .

_____

_____

_____

■ In the first instance, the writer takes one example (somebody transferring from Marketing to Data Processing) and then describes the example as a trend. I hope we can agree that you need to have more than one example to point to before you can truthfully call it a trend.

■ In the second example, the writer turns what was only an 'opinion' in the first sentence into a 'fact' in the second.

As a writer, your aim should be to write briefly, clearly and honestly.

As a reader, you should be on the look-out for this kind of slippery language, where words are being used to distort ideas.

The main reason for making sure that you write briefly and clearly is that it will be easier for your readers to understand. Simple words and short sentences are a useful part of this, but it is possible to go too far.

Activity 23

■ Time guide 3 minutes

What impression does this notice make on you?

■ The holiday list is now on the board.

Please decide what holidays you want to take. Make sure your holiday plans do not clash with other people's. Check this with your Section Head. You have until the end of the month. Only Section Heads may enter dates on the list.

You are advised to fix your dates early. If you do not, you may not be able to take the weeks you want. If you do need to change your dates later, we will try to help. However, this may be difficult. You should see your Section Head in the first instance.

_____

_____

_____

Different people may get different impressions, but to my mind, the exaggerated simplicity of this notice says:

■ this person is talking down to me;

■ he or she is treating me like a child or a halfwit.

Do you agree that it has a 'children's book' quality? 'The cat sat on the mat. She is called Sam. Sam the cat is black' – and so on.

To others it may sound harsh and impersonal, like a sergeant major instructing his platoon.

Either way, it shows that using a series of simple sentences has its drawbacks. Not every reader needs the same level of simplicity, and obviously some can cope with a good deal more complexity:

● longer words;

● longer sentences;

● more complicated ideas.

The point is to get it right for your particular audience, and here are two extracts from daily newspapers to show what I mean. They covered the same story on the same day, but in a very different style.

The Mirror	The Independent
Curious kid in Rambo carnage	**Gun law review after N Z massacre**
A little boy's curiosity cost him his life as he cycled after police cars racing through his village. The six year-old rode into the sights of crazed gunman David Gray who shot him dead. Gray finally died in a hail of police bullets. Some of his victims are thought to have been young-sters attending a children's party nearby. The gun-mad loner blasted police with two automatic rifles before being cornered in a house.	Eleven people were killed during 23 hours of terror in Aramoana (population about 50) by a local man described as a loner who liked to wear paramilitary uniforms and had a passion for guns. The gunman, David Gray, 33 is thought to have used an AK-47 semi-automatic rifle and the government immediately said it would review the gun laws in New Zealand, where the possesion of such weapons is allowed. The dead included a boy aged six and a police sergeant. Police said two people were still unaccounted for.

The *Daily Mirror* is a popular 'tabloid', while the *Independent* is an up-market 'broadsheet'. The editors of these two papers have a fairly clear idea of what sort of people read them, and what sort of language to use when writing for them.

The *Independent*'s readers would feel that they were being talked down to if they were addressed in the racy style the *Mirror* normally uses; while the *Mirror*'s readers would probably feel annoyed to have to work through the sort of sober language used by the *Independent*.

Of course, the choice of different language for different readerships is no accident, and there are ways of measuring just what kind of language is being used.

**5.1
A reading index**

To give a little more precision to our measurement of how easy to read our writing is we can use a reading index. There are various reading indices which one can use but here is a very simple one.

Take a passage of 100 words.

Here is an example.

'Thank you for your letter of 4 *January* in which you expressed an *interest* in the post of first line *supervisor* in our plant.

We feel that your *experience* and *qualifications* may be what we are looking for and we should be very pleased to discuss the post with you.

I suggest we meet here on Friday 1 *February* at 11 a.m. when my colleague Mr Paul, who will be Process *Manager* of the new plant, will be able to join our *discussion*.

Please let me know if this date is not *convenient*, so we can arrange an *alternative*.'

First, you count the number of sentences and work out the average number of words per sentence. You do this by working out the sum:

100 divided by the number of sentences.

Activity 24

Part
B

■ Time guide 1 minute

How many sentences are there in this passage? _____

So the average sentence length is $\frac{100}{?} =$ _____ .

There are four sentences in the passage so the average sentence length is:

$$\frac{100}{4} = 25 \text{ words.}$$

Next, you count up the number of words which contain three or more syllables in a group of 100 words. As you can see, I have underlined the ten words of three or more syllables in this passage.

(You notice that I have not included 'expressed' in the first line of the passage, which you could argue is a three-syllable word. This is because you don't include in your calculations any words which only become three syllables because they end in 'ing', 'ed' or 'es'.)

Finally you add together

| The average number of words in a sentence | + | Number of words of three or more syllables in a group of 100 words |

and this gives you the *readability index*.

So, in the example we're looking at we add:

$$25 + 10 = 35.$$

The reading index for this passage is 35, which is about right for a simple business letter. If the reading index for any passage falls between 35 and 45 you can feel fairly confident that the reading level is suitable for most business purposes.

Activity 25

■ Time guide 10 minutes

Work out the reading index for this passage (adapted from 'What strategy?' by Dr F. Metcalfe, *Training and Development*, Vol. 3, No. 8, December 1984). The words containing three or more syllables have already been highlighted.

'To counter the *hideous spectacle* of high and growing *unemployment* the only *solutions* offered seem to be 'get on your bike', a shorter working week or a shorter working life. Leaving aside the *unrealism* of the first, the others appear to me (*respectively*) a *formula* for *overtime* payments or a *rejection* into *another* kind of *unemployment* called early *retirement*. Why, oh why, isn't the power of the training *industry* marshalled to tackle the problem of the long-term *unemployed*, that increasing army of those robbed of *dignity* and hope? Training by its very nature *inculcates* increased skill and *awareness* and *confidence*.'

I make the reading index for that passage 43 – in other words near the top of the scale of what we can reasonbly expect to understand without some difficulty.

Of course, you won't have time to apply a readability index to everything you write but it might be quite useful and informative to try it on a few samples of your writing – particularly if you suspect that your style is rather long-winded.

Looking at the reading index confirms that reasonably short sentences and simple words makes our writing easy to understand, but we want it to be a bit more than that. We also want it to be *pleasing* to read.

Activity 26

■ Time guide 3 minutes

Look at this passage. It is brief and simple but the overall effect is of a rather boring piece of writing. Jot down why you think this is.

'Darlington is a town in North East England. It has a population of 96,000. It is just north of the boundary between Durham and North Yorkshire. Its heyday was in the nineteenth century. It grew with the development of railways in the region. Traditional heavy engineering has now been replaced by light engineering plants and service industries. Unemployment is higher than the national average. It has tended to be less hard hit by recession than the surrounding areas.'

_____

_____

_____

_____

_____

Well, what is 'boring' tends to be a rather personal judgement, but I hope we can agree that this passage isn't very interesting to read because it doesn't flow. The sentences are all of a rather similar length and none of them connects with the sentence which follows, which tends to create a rather jumpy effect. This is partly due to the repetition of 'It . . . It . . . It . . .'.

So, though being careful not to make the sentences too long, we can improve this passage if we run sentences together to make the whole thing flow better:

'Darlington is just north of the boundary between Durham and North Yorkshire, in North East England. It has a population of 96,000. It grew with the development of railways in the region and reached its heyday in the nineteenth century. Now traditional heavy engineering has been replaced by light engineering plants and service industries. Although unemployment there is higher than the national average it has tended to be less hard hit by recession than the surrounding areas.'

I hope you agree that this version reads better than the original.

Notice too that the length of sentences varies more this time. If we count up the words in each sentence in this version we find that they go like this:

16, 6, 18, 14, 23.

This variety in sentence length and structure makes any written material more interesting to read.

I am not suggesting that you should count up the number of words per sentence when you are writing and make sure that the same number doesn't recur too often! But if you have to write a fairly lengthy piece, a long letter or a report for instance, you **should** be able to make it more interesting reading if you deliberately vary the sentence length and structure somewhat.

Activity 27

■ Time guide 10 minutes

Here is another example of rather monotonous writing.

Write a version of your own which flows better and in which the sentence length is more varied.

'Supervisors have always tended to be the 'best' operatives.

This is tradition.

One example is promoting the salesman with the highest turnover to sales supervisor.

Another example is promoting the best toolmaker to toolroom foreman.

Their previous position gives them a special understanding of the problems of the people they now supervise.

Supervisors also need to be able to manage people. Being good at one kind of job doesn't necessarily mean they'll be good at another.

You need training.'

_____

_____

_____

_____

_____

_____

_____

_____

_____

_____

It's very unlikely that our improved versions of that passage are the same. But here is mine anyway to compare with yours.

'Traditionally, supervisors have tended to be the 'best' operatives. Thus, the salesman with the highest turnover is promoted to sales supervisor and the best toolmaker is promoted to toolroom foreman. Although their previous position gives them a special understanding of the problems of the people they now supervise, being good at one job doesn't necessarily mean they'll be good at another. For supervisors need to be able to manage people and for that they need training.'

I think you'll agree that this (and yours too I hope) is more varied and flows better than the original.

Writing simple, clear letters, memos and reports which read well will do a lot to improve our reputation for communicating well but, as we mentioned at the beginning of this part of the unit, we may still feel that what we write sounds rather cold and impersonal. So how can we get round that problem?

Let's look at a few simple techniques we could use.

**6.1
People matter
more than things**

Look at this pair of sentences.

'Every effort will be made.'

'We shall make every effort.'

In the first sentence the emphasis is on the ***effort*** – that is the main idea which we register if we read that sentence. In the second sentence the emphasis is spread between 'we' and 'effort' so we learn from that sentence what is being made ('every effort') and who is doing it ('we').

Sometimes, of course, we ***want*** to emphasize a thing rather than a person but, as a general rule, if you write in this impersonal way for any length, you create a rather cold, remote effect which doesn't give a very favourable impression.

Activity 28

■ Time guide 3 minutes

Here are two more sentences written in a similar way to the one we've just looked at. Rewrite each sentence so that the emphasis is on the person as much as on the thing. I've given you a start on the first one.

■ Enquiries will be dealt with by Miss Smith.

Miss Smith will _____

■ Your application has been received by the Personnel Officer.

_____

_____

I would have completed the sentences as follows.

Miss Smith will deal with enquiries. The Personnel Officer has received your application.

Your wording may not be quite the same as mine but I hope it is on the same lines.

Perhaps you can see what I mean about the rather cold, remote effect created by writing which emphasizes ***things*** as opposed to ***people*** when you read the following.

Dear Sir

Your letter of 10 January has been passed to the Editorial Section.

Fees are not normally paid but, in this instance, it is felt that consideration should be given to the particular expenses incurred by you as a result of your research. A decision on this, however, will be made by the Editor and will be conveyed to you within a few days.

Your contribution to the journal is appreciated.

Yours faithfully

Activity 29

■ Time guide 5 minutes

Rewrite this letter, making sure that the *people* involved are emphasized as much as things like 'fees' and 'decisions', as we did in the previous activity.

Remember also what we have said earlier about writing simply; there's quite a bit of room for improvement in this letter.

_____

_____

_____

_____

_____

_____

_____

_____

_____

_____

My version of the letter looks like this; there will almost certainly be some differences between yours and mine in the choice of wording. However, I hope you find that yours and mine sound more human than the original.

> Dear Sir
>
> Thank you for your letter of 10 January which I have passed to the Editorial Section.
>
> We do not normally pay fees but, in this instance, will consider the particular expenses which you have incurred during your research. This, however, this will be the Editor's decision which I shall let you know within a few days.
>
> Thank you very much for your contribution to the journal.
>
> Yours faithfully

**6.2
Don't hide
behind the firm**

If you look again at my version of the letter in the last activity, you will see that I have used 'I' and 'we' rather than saying 'the Journal', or 'the company', or something similarly anonymous. Thus the second paragraph begins:

'We do not normally pay fees',

and not

'The journal does not normally pay fees'.

This is another way in which we can make what we write sound as though it were written by one human being to another.

I realize that this may not always be easy. Your company may have a house style for letters which makes it difficult for you to use 'I' and 'we' even if you would like to.

And, more than that, you may feel that if you use 'I' you are leaving yourself rather exposed to some personal comeback from what you are writing. But usually the risk isn't that great.

Let's look again for a moment at the last letter we wrote. Here's my version of it again:

> Dear Sir
>
> Thank you for your letter of 10 January which I have passed to the Editorial Section.
>
> We do not normally pay fees but, in this instance, will consider the particular expenses which you have incurred during your research. This, however, will be the Editor's decision and I shall let you know what he decides within a few days.
>
> Thank you very much for your contribution to the journal.
>
> Yours faithfully

This says that 'I' have passed the letter to the Editorial Section and 'I' will let the correspondent know the Editor's decision within a few days. Neither of those statements is very controversial or likely to get the writer into difficulties.

Everywhere else in the letter I have used 'we', which suggests that it has the backing of the whole organization but still sounds reasonably friendly. As far as **meaning** is concerned there is very little difference between 'We do not normally pay fees', and 'It is not normally company policy to pay fees', but there is a considerable difference in the attitude.

Extension 3 If you have to write letters and memos as part of your job, I suggest that you look at *The Janner Letterwriter* by G. Janner, M.P.

Activity 30

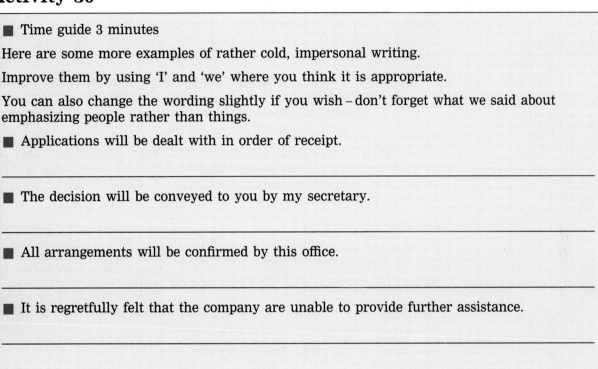

■ Time guide 3 minutes

Here are some more examples of rather cold, impersonal writing.

Improve them by using 'I' and 'we' where you think it is appropriate.

You can also change the wording slightly if you wish – don't forget what we said about emphasizing people rather than things.

■ Applications will be dealt with in order of receipt.

_____

■ The decision will be conveyed to you by my secretary.

_____

■ All arrangements will be confirmed by this office.

_____

■ It is regretfully felt that the company are unable to provide further assistance.

_____

_____

Here is how I should rewrite each of these sentences. Of course, your version may differ slightly from mine.

■ We shall deal with applications in the order we receive them.

■ My secretary will let you know the decision.

■ We shall confirm all arrangements.

■ I'm sorry that we're no longer able to help./I'm sorry that we can't help any further.

**6.3
Technical reports –
an exception**

There is one possible exception to what we've said about it being preferable to write emphasizing the person rather than concentrating entirely on what's being done. That is if you are writing a technical report.

For a long time, it has been common to write reports in a form which didn't actually mention yourself. Thus you would say:

'Clocking-on procedure was observed 14 times.'

rather than

'I observed clocking-on procedure 14 times.'

Once you get used to writing in this impersonal way, it's still possible to write something clear, interesting and lively which doesn't sound as though it was produced by a robot, but it's something which many people find difficult.

Extension 4 If you are required to write technical and other reports you may find it useful to study the relevant chapters in *Mastering Business Communications*, by L. A. Woolcott and W. R. Unwin.

If you are writing a fairly straightforward report (perhaps in the form of a memo) to your immediate boss, I think I would still use 'I' rather than writing in an impersonal form. Unless, of course, there is a rule in your company about writing reports in this way.

I think

'I discussed the proposals fully with the entire workteam in B section and we reached the following conclusions . . .'

sounds just as clear and efficient and more human than

'The proposals were fully discussed with the workteam in B section and the following conclusions were reached . . .'.

And most people find it easier to write referring directly to themselves, too.

**6.4
The personal touch**

Finally, we can often make what we write sound more human if we spend a few moments adding a personal touch – even to an everyday memo.

I ***don't*** mean by this that we should write in a gossipy style like this:

'I observed clocking-on on the nightshift 14 times. Jolly cold it was too! Still, here are the results anyway.'

■ Time guide 2 minutes

But look at these two memos.

Both convey the same information, but which would you prefer to have? Which do you think would create a more favourable impression with the people receiving it?

Memorandum	
From: A. Briggs Quality Circle Leader	To: Quality Circle Members
Subject: Machine downtime project meeting	Date: 1 June

The next meeting to discuss the machine downtime project will be this Thursday 2.00 pm in the Committee Room. Please let me know if you are unable to attend.

A. B.

Memorandum	
From: A. Briggs Quality Circle Leader	To: Quality Circle Members
Subject: Machine downtime project meeting	Date: 1 June

Thank you for the encouraging response to this project which I've received since the last meeting.

The next meeting will be on Thursday 2.00 pm in the Committee Room when I hope we can discuss your findings more fully.

Please let me know if you are unable to attend and I'll make sure you are kept informed of developments.

A. B.

I think the second memo sounds friendlier and more encouraging, yet the effort to write a memo like that rather than the first one takes only a minute or two.

Sometimes the addition of a single sentence is enough to achieve the same effect:

- 'Thank you for your letter of...';
- 'Thank you for your support.';
- 'I look forward to seeing you at the next meeting on...';
- 'Please let me know if I can be...';
- 'If you need any further help please...'.

Any of these may be suitable to assure whoever you are writing to that *you* are human and that you realize *they* are too.

And, once you get into the habit of including a comment like these, it becomes an almost automatic response and not something over which you have to chew your pen for hours!

Activity 32

■ Time guide 5 minutes

Here are the texts of two memos.

I've left plenty of space around the text for you to add a few words or a sentence which you feel would make them both sound more personal and more likely to get a favourable response from the readers.

Memorandum	

From: B. Johnson
        Supervisor
	To: S. Wooley
	      Q. C. Manager

Subject: Staff Turnover	Date: 7 May

Here is the analysis of staff turnover May 1980–December 1984 in my section.

I am still waiting for data from personnel for the remaining period.

B. J.

Memorandum	
From: John Evans Training Officer	To: Supervisors
Subject: Training plans	Date: 2 Nov.

Following our meeting I have drawn up training proposals for your section. Copies, which have also been sent to section superintendents, are attached.

J. E.

Here is how I would change these two memos to give them a more personal touch.

Memorandum	
From: B. Johnson Supervisor	To: S. Wooley Q. C. Manager
Subject: Staff Turnover	Date: 7 May

Here is the analysis of staff turnover May 1980–December 1984 in my section.

I am still waiting for data from personnel for the remaining period and will let you have the figures as soon as they are available.

B. J.

Memorandum	
From: John Evans Training Officer	To: Supervisors
Subject: Training Plans	Date: 2 Nov

Thank you for your contribution to the meeting last week. I have now drawn up training proposals for your sections and shall be glad to discuss them with you. Copies, which have also been sent to section superintendents, are attached.

J. E.

What you do to *make* these memos seem more personal is obviously a matter of individual judgement, but I hope we can agree that much that we write in business is improved by making it clear that there was a human being behind it.

You might find it useful to answer the following Self Check questions now before we go on to look at getting our ideas organized when we write.

■ Time guide 15 minutes

Here is another string of long-winded expressions. Try to come up with **one**, or perhaps **two**, words which could replace them.

1. Establish a connection between _____

2. Pay due attention to _____

3. In the vicinity of _____

4. Reach a consensus _____

5. Under no circumstances whatsoever _____

6. At every available opportunity _____

7. Without the slightest reservation _____

8. Arrive at the conclusion _____

9. Reach the decision _____

10. It may well be that _____

11. With a fair degree of probability _____

12. Unable to proceed further _____

13. In addition _____

14. Poorly illuminated _____

15. Socially withdrawn and inhibited _____

16. At the present moment in time _____

17. Render assistance to _____

18. Provide the necessary resources _____

19. On a subsequent occasion _____

20. Ascertain the location of _____

In each of the three following statements one idea has been expressed twice. Cross out whatever words you think are unnecessary.

21. Manning levels will continue to remain the same.

22. I may possibly go home soon.

23. He tentatively suggested the following changes.

continued overleaf

Read the following statements. Why is the writer 'cheating'?

24. It is a well-known fact that men tire more quickly than women in routine manufacturing operations. Therefore we should employ . . .

25. It is generally agreed that overtime working is unavoidable, and since this is so . . .

26. Several changes have been made in the layout of the Production Department. These improvements have enabled us to establish a small packing area . . .

27. Rewrite the following passage so that the writer is not 'hiding behind' the company.

The company does not normally deal directly with the public and it is usually recommended that you contact the retailer first. However, since the problem is urgent, a replacement unit will be sent to you directly from this office.

_____

_____

_____

_____

_____

Response check 2

The expressions could be written more simply like this:

1. LINK
2. NOTE
3. NEAR
4. AGREE
5. NEVER
6. WHENEVER
7. DEFINITELY
8. CONCLUDE
9. DECIDE
10. PROBABLY
11. LIKELY
12. STUCK
13. ALSO
14. DIM
15. SHY
16. NOW
17. HELP
18. EQUIP
19. LATER
20. FIND
21. You could cross out either 'continue to' or 'remain'.
22. Cross out 'possibly' – if you *may* go home soon it's only a possibility anyway.
23. Cross out 'tentatively' – a suggestion is tentative in any case.
24. The writer suggests that the argument is well-supported ('It is a well-known fact'), but doesn't give any evidence for this.
25. Same criticism as for Question 24. There's no evidence given that overtime working is unavoidable.
26. The writer refers to 'changes' as 'improvements' without showing us why they were improvements.
27. Your wording may differ slightly from mine:

    'We do not normally deal directly with the public but suggest you contact the retailer first. However, since the problem is urgent, we will send you a replacement unit directly.'

- Accuracy, brevity and clarity are the basis of effective writing.

- Correct spelling and grammar are important for the writer's credibility. Watch out for:

  - apostrophe-S used instead of a plural;

  - wrong use of *its* and *it's*;

  - spelling of longer and more unusual words.

- You can make your writing simple, clear and direct by:

  - avoiding lengthy, overworked words and phrases;

  - using your own words rather than what is currently fashionable;

  - avoiding saying the same thing twice;

  - writing honestly.

- To sustain the reader's interest in your writing you should:

  - write fairly short sentences;

  - but vary sentence length and structure.

- To measure how easy to understand your writing is you can apply a reading index to a passage of 100 words. Simple business writing should have an index between 35 and 45.

- To make your writing sound human you should:

  - emphasize the people in your sentences rather than the things (i.e. write actively rather than passively);

  - use 'I' and 'we' rather than writing impersonally (with the possible exception of technical reports);

  - try to include a personal touch – a recognition of the reader's involvement – when writing memos and letters.

GETTING YOUR IDEAS ORGANIZED

1   Introduction

So far we've looked at why we write and the circumstances in which we might need to write. Also how we can write in a simple, correct and friendly way so that the reader understands what we are saying and, we hope, responds favourably.

But simple, straightforward writing alone isn't enough if our thinking is muddled. So, finally, we must look at how we can organize our ideas and then lay out what we're writing in a way which makes it easy for the reader to see the plan behind it.

2   Why am I doing this?

To start to organize our thinking, when we know we have to write something (perhaps a letter, report or memo) the first thing we must do is ask ourselves *why* we are writing it. What is the purpose of what we are about to write?

This need only take seconds – it doesn't mean that you gloomily have to review the whole of your working life!

Activity 33

■ Time guide 4 minutes

Look at these written messages.

Jot down what you think the purpose of each one is.

(a)

Telephone Message

Time received: 11.20   Date: 11/12

From: H. Williams—Hay Engineering 67694

The ARAC14 bearings were despatched by road this a.m.
Should arrive before noon tomorrow.

Received by: R. E.

(b)

Memorandum	
From: Office Supervisor	To: All Office Staff
Subject: Holiday Timetable	Date: 1st Feb

I should like to complete the holiday timetable for this year by the
end of the week.

Would you please complete the attached form and return it to me
by Friday. Please see me if there are any problems.

Thanks.

R. H.

continued overleaf

(c)

> **Safety Guide**
>
> 3.   ... must be thoroughly understood by each employee.
>
> 4.   **Notification**
>
>   The supervisor in charge of an area where an emergency occurs is reponsible for ensuring that his immediate superior is notified as soon as possible. The superintendent will ensure that the Departmental Manager, Safety Engineer and Plant Engineer are notified.
>
> 5.   **Security Guard Functions**
>
>   Because the guard must remain at the factory entrance ...

(d)

> 10.00
>
> **Jack**
>
> Would you let me have the staff absence figures for the last quarter for your section by this evening please. It's getting urgent.
>
>   **Susan**

You may have noticed other points but I think the ***purpose*** of them is that the telephone message and safety guide are giving information and the memo and Susan's note are asking for information.

I think you'll find that anything we write comes in one or both of these categories – we are giving information or asking the reader to give us information or to make some other kind of response.

Once you are clear about your purpose it is time to think briefly about who your readers will be. This will help you make sure you use the right sort of language to put your information across.

So, if we're giving information we next have to ask ourselves: 'How much does the reader need to know?'

Activity 34

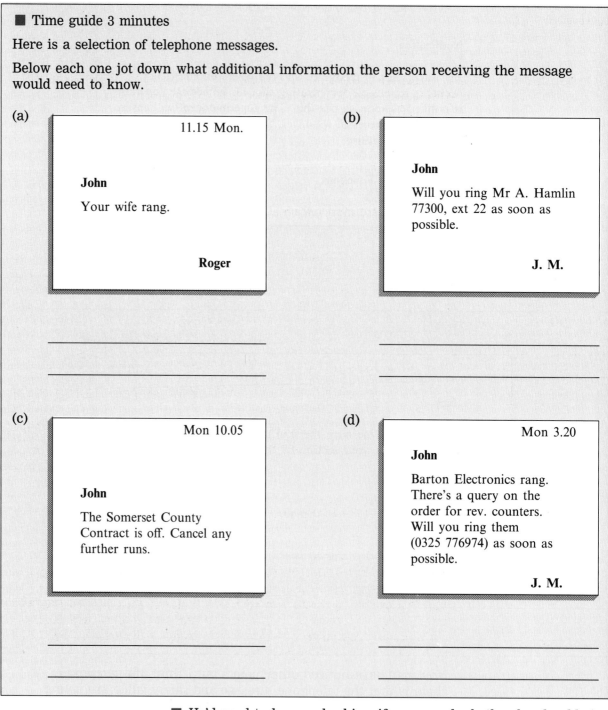

■ Time guide 3 minutes

Here is a selection of telephone messages.

Below each one jot down what additional information the person receiving the message would need to know.

(a)

> 11.15 Mon.
>
> John
> Your wife rang.
>
> Roger

(b)

> John
> Will you ring Mr A. Hamlin 77300, ext 22 as soon as possible.
>
> J. M.

(c)

> Mon 10.05
>
> John
> The Somerset County Contract is off. Cancel any further runs.

(d)

> Mon 3.20
> John
> Barton Electronics rang. There's a query on the order for rev. counters. Will you ring them (0325 776974) as soon as possible.
>
> J. M.

■ He'd need to know why his wife rang and whether he should ring her back.

■ He'd need to know when the message about Mr Hamlin was received and what he is supposed to ring back about. It's possible also that a name and number may not mean a lot to John – he should be told the name of the company too.

■ He'd need to know who this message about the Somerset County contract was from and who had received the message.

■ He'd need to know who to telephone at Barton Electronics.

So we can see that none of those telephone messages is altogether efficient and a few moments thought by the person taking the telephone call could save quite a bit of wasted time.

Taking telephone messages is one of the most elementary kinds of writing that we have to do at work. Often, we'd expect to have to give rather more thought to deciding how much the reader needed to know, though the principle remains the same.

Activity 35

■ Time guide 5 minutes

Suppose you have to write a report on the success, or lack of it, of introducing flexible working hours into your section. You will have to mention:

■ any increase or loss of productivity;

■ any difficulties you have found in running the flexible-hours system;

■ your analysis of the attitudes of your workteam to the new system.

You have all the information you need to hand, but what do you need to know before you start to write? Jot down *two* points on which you would have to be clear before you started writing.

_____

_____

_____

_____

Our answers to this may vary, but I suggest that you would need to know:

■ who was going to read your report (presumably you would give it to your immediate boss, but the kind of information you would include would depend on who *else* was going to read it or what use was going to be made of it);

■ how much your readers already know about the subject.
For instance, are they likely to be familiar with the precise flexible-hours system you've been operating or do you need to describe it in some detail?

So, if we're giving information, we need to know who it's for and how much the reader already knows about the subject. Even if you feel confident that the reader will be fairly familiar with what you're going to say, it still helps if you jog his memory with a brief introductory sentence, or (if it's a report) a short paragraph which sums up the work done to date.

Here are some examples of what I mean:

Dear Sir

Interactive Video Training

I was interested to read of the development of . . .

Memorandum	
From: Production Manager	To: All Supervisors
Subject: Mechanized Production Scheduling	Date: 1st June

Further to our meeting with G. Thomas last week at which we agreed to use the computer for production scheduling from the 1st July, he has arranged a series of training sessions for all production personnel . . .

2.2 Asking for a response

If the purpose of our writing is to get a response from the readers, then we need to make it as straightforward as possible for them to do what we want.

For example, suppose you have a workteam of 30 people and you are trying to arrange the holiday timetable so that you have enough staff to cover at all times.

30 people's holiday requirements are too complicated to scribble down on the back of an envelope! And you would be left with quite a time-consuming analysis of dates if you just asked them all to write down the dates they required.

Moreover, they will be more likely to respond if you give them each a form showing all the dates available and asking them just to tick the weeks they would like.

2.3 Encouraging a response

Sometimes it isn't really practicable to provide for people to respond in this way, but you can often at least *encourage* the response you want in a few words.

Here's an example of what I mean.

Suppose, to complete your records, you need some figures from various departments in your company. You send out a memo to the departments involved. You are *more* likely to get the response you want if your memo ends

'Please let me know if there will be any difficulty providing the figures by Friday'

than if you simply ask for the information by Friday, because you have given an *encouragement* to the reader to respond.

Of course, in practice you would probably *still* find yourself telephoning slow departments or having to go round them in person on Friday afternoon!

Activity 36

■ Time guide 8 minutes

Here are three different situations in which you have to ask somebody to do something. In each one you want to encourage a particular response.

On the blank memo form for each one, write the text of the memo. (You'll see that the details at the top have already been filled in.) Each memo needs to be only *two* or *three* sentences long.

(a) You want to know numbers being set to a training session on new products. You are aiming to get three people from each supervisor's section. The sessions will be held on 2 April – details have already been circulated. The cost of training is charged out to user departments.

(b) You are the safety representative for your plant and you are letting supervisors know when you want to make a regular safety inspection in their area. As you haven't had the job long you really want the supervisors to join you on the inspection and point out any possible hazards or problems they have come across.

(c) You are secretary of your company's Welfare Association. Attendance at committee meetings is often poor and you want to get a better turn-out at the next meeting in the canteen on 9 April at 7 p.m. You want to be sure that every department is represented and wonder whether, if the usual representatives can't come, they could arrange for somebody else to.

(a)

Memorandum	
From: Training Officer	To: All Supervisors
Subject: Product Knowledge Training	Date: 8 March

continued overleaf

(b)

Memorandum	
From: Safety Representative	To: All Supervisors
Subject: Safety Inspection	Date: 11 Feb.

(c)

Memorandum	
From: Association Secretary – Welfare	To: All Supervisors
Subject: W. A. Committee Meeting	Date: 1 Apr.

Here is what I would write for each of those memos. Quite possibly we have used different ways of encouraging the response we wanted. That doesn't matter. I hope we can agree though that giving a few moments' thought to *how* you can encourage a response is more likely to result in an *effective* piece of communication.

(a)

Memorandum	
From: Training Officer	To: All Supervisors
Subject: Production Knowledge Training	Date: 8 March

I need to finalize numbers for the training sessions on new products on 2 April, details of which I sent you last week.

I should be grateful if you would let me know definite numbers by Friday. If I don't hear from you I'll assume you are sending three people from your section and will charge out accordingly.

B. P.

(b)

Memorandum	
From: Safety Representative	To: All Supervisors
Subject: Safety Inspection	Date: 11 Feb.

I should like to make a routine safety inspection in each area of the plant next Monday morning, 16 February.

I should be very grateful if you would spare the time to join me on the inspection and should welcome any suggestions or problems you are able to point out.

A. B.

(c)

Memorandum	
From: Secretary – Welfare Association	To: All Supervisors
Subject: W. A. Committee Meeting	Date: 1 Apr.

The next meeting of the Welfare Association Committee will be held on Thursday 9 April at 7.00 pm in the canteen.

I do hope you will be able to attend. If you are **not** able to do so this time, perhaps you would ask somebody from your department to come instead of you.

It would be very helpful if you would let me know by Friday who will be coming from your department.

K. B.

3   Structure

So, having decided what is the basic purpose of whatever we're writing, and thought in terms of who we are giving information to and why, or what we want them to do, we are finally left with the problem of how to put the writing together – the structure.

This isn't a problem if we are writing something very brief, but it can take a bit more thinking about if we have to handle several items of information. And usually, that thinking process, getting our own ideas in order, will take care of the structure.

Here's an example of what I mean.

3.1 Grouping

Imagine that we run a large hotel with conference facilities. Here is a list, arranged alphabetically, of the services which we can provide in the conference rooms.

Back projection systems	– available at an additional charge
Blackboard and easel	– provided inclusive of room hire
Flip chart, pads and pens	– provided inclusive of room hire
Free-standing lectern	– " " " " "
Fruit squash	– " " " " "
Iced water	– " " " " "
Mineral water	– " " " " "
Mints	– " " " " "
35 mm slide projector	– available at an additional price
16 mm sound projector	– " " " " "
Overhead projector	– provided inclusive of room hire
Pads and pencils	– provided inclusive of room hire
P. A. system	– available at an additional price
Photocopying	– available at an additional price
Secretarial service	– " " " " "
Telex	– " " " " "

Looking at this list would certainly tell you what facilities are available, but could it be organized more helpfully–could it be better structured?

Activity 37

■ Time guide 5 minutes

Jot down how you would reorganize the list so that it was more use to a client reading it. (There's no need to write out all the items on the list.)

_____

_____

_____

_____

_____

_____

_____

I hope we can agree that, although the list *is* organized in one way (it is alphabetically arranged), it isn't very useful as it stands.

I would reorganize it like this, separating items which are included in the room hire from those for which an additional charge is made. Notice also that I would group drinks and mints under one heading – 'Refreshments'.

Facilities provided inclusive of room hire

Blackboard and easel
Flip chart, pad and pens
Free-standing lectern
Overhead projector
Pads and pencils
Refreshments – fruit squash, iced water, mineral water, mints

Facilities provided at an additional price

Back projection system
35 mm slide projector
16 mm sound projector
P. A. system
Photocopying
Secretarial service
Telex

And this is basically how we structure any amount of information which we have to write down for somebody else.

Group items which belong together: put them together under a heading which makes clear what that section is about.

What isn't clear from the last activity, though, is one other important stage in our organization.

Activity 38

■ Time guide 3 minutes

Suppose we are writing a letter to a client explaining what the hotel's conference facilities are, the costs and the dates on which they are available. We have already grouped the items under these headings.

---

24 hour conference package

■ Special deal available from January 1, 24 hour conference package includes full use of conference facilities and accommodation in single rooms with private bathroom, breakfast, coffee, lunch, tea, dinner at £8 per head – strongly recommended.

Costs

■ Conference suite is hired per **part day** (maximum 5 hours)
      or per **whole day** (maximum 12 hours)
■ Whole, one third or two thirds of conference suite may be hired – price list available
■ Seminar rooms hired separately – £15 per **part day each**
          £20 per **whole day each**
Coffee, tea, buffet, lunch, dinner available. Five possible menus – menus with price per head available.

Dates available

■ 20 October, 27 October
■ 14 November
■ Any date after 12 January

Conference facilities

■ Conference suite – conference room 54′ 6″ × 17′ 6″ with own cloakroom and toilet
■ Can be divided into 2 or 3 smaller rooms
■ 12 small seminar rooms each seating 12 people
■ Some equipment included in room hire – list available
■ Additional services charged separately – list available

What decision would you have to make about the groups of information before you could write the letter?

_____

_____

_____

_____

You would have to decide *which order* to put them in.

In almost all business writing you start with the most important item and work down to the least important. Most people who are at work feel they have more than enough paperwork to read, and if you didn't make the important points early, they might never read far enough to find them.

Sometimes there isn't one group of information which is clearly more important than another. (You may think that is the case in the example we're looking at. Costs, available dates or the facilities available could *each* be the most important factor to the reader – it depends what the particular circumstances are.)

Usually, however, there is one group of information which has to come first, if what is to follow is to make sense to the reader. That is probably the case in the example we're looking at.

Activity 39

■ Time guide 3 minutes

Jot down the order in which you would deal with the groups of information in your letter to the client.

(You need only write down the heading for each group.)

_____

_____

_____

_____

This is the order in which I would deal with the information in the letter:

■ conference facilities;

■ costs;

■ 24 hour conference package;

■ dates available.

When you make a choice like this, obviously some personal judgement enters into it, but I hope we can agree that the letter wouldn't make much sense unless we first explained what conference facilities we could offer.

If you glance back at the groups of information about the hotel's conference facilities you will notice that, within each group, the items of information are already in a logical order and it should be fairly straightforward to use them as the basis for a letter.

Often, of course, individual items of information will still be jumbled up even after we have sorted them into groups.

Here is an example.

Conference facilities

Conference suite has its own cloakroom and toilets

Conference suite is called the Penshaw Suite

It can be divided into two or three smaller rooms

The conference room can seat 120

(A) There are 12 syndicate rooms

If the conference suite is divided the dimensions are:
two thirds room 36' x 17'6" x 10'
one third room 18' x 17' 6" x 10'

(A) Each syndicate room seats 12

The conference room can accommodate 100 for a buffet or 80 for lunch or dinner

(A) Each syndicate room has its own bathroom

But the principle for organizing the information is the same.

We group items which belong together and then arrange them in order of importance. And to save writing a lot of information out again we can often do this by simply putting a letter of the alphabet beside items which belong together.

I've already put 'A' beside points referring to syndicate rooms.

Activity 40

■ Time guide 2 minutes

Put a letter (B, C or D) against any items on the list of conference facilities which you think belong together.

In this example I would say that these topics are covered (the letters beside them are the letters I used):

The conference suite	(B)
The dimensions	(C)
The seating capacity	(D)
The syndicate rooms	(A)

My list of the conference facilities would be as below. Check your letters with mine but don't worry if they do not entirely match – we may just have taken a different view of the information.

Conference facilities	Group
Conference suite has its own cloakroom and toilets	B2
Conference suite is called the Penshaw Suite	B1
It can be divided into two or three smaller rooms	B3
The conference room measures 54' 6" x 17' 6" x 10'	C1
The conference room can seat 120	D1
There are 12 syndicate rooms	A1
If the conference suite is divided the dimensions are: two thirds room 36' x 17' 6" x 10' one third room 18' x 17' 6" x 10'	C2
Each syndicate room seats 12	A2
The conference room can accommodate 100 for a buffet or 80 for lunch or dinner	D2
Each syndicate room has its own bathroom	A3

You can see if you look at my list that within each letter group, A, B, C, D, I have now added a number to each item. That shows the order in which I would make each of those points as I was writing the letter.

So, if we take group B which contains the following points:

Conference suite has its own cloakroom and toilets	B2
Conference suite is called the Penshaw Suite	B1
It can be divided into 2 or 3 smaller rooms	B3

I should write them up something like this:

'Our conference room, which is called the Penshaw Suite, has its own cloakroom and toilets and can be divided into two or three smaller rooms if required.'

Activity 41

■ Time guide 1 minute

Look again at your list of points about the hotel's conference facilities and jot down the order in which you would deal with each letter.

My list would start with 'B'.

My list would be like this: B; C; D; A; though it is possible to do it in other ways.

Having decided that, I should write the information up something like this.

> Our conference room, the Penshaw Suite, has its own cloakroom and toilets and can be divided into two or three smaller rooms as required.
>
> The whole room measures 54' 6" x 17' 6" x 10'.
>
> But when divided, the two thirds room provides accomodation measuring 36' x 17' 6" x 10' and the one third room provides accommodation measuring 18' x 17' 6" x 10'.
>
> The Penshaw Suite seats 120 people for meetings, a maximum of 100 for buffet service or 80 for lunch or dinner.
>
> We also have 12 syndicate rooms, each seating 12 people and each with its own bathroom.

Activity 42

■ Time guide 10 minutes

Here is a list of points about the *24 hour conference package*.

24 hour conference package	
Full use of conference facilities Strongly recommended Accommodation in single rooms with private bathrooms Coffee and tea are provided during conference Price includes full English breakfast, lunch and dinner Available from January 1st Price is £44 per head Single rooms have colour television, radio, telephone, tea and coffee making facilities and mini bar Represents extremely good value for money	

■ Letter the points which belong together (using A, B, C, D).

■ Decide the order in which you would write up the points in each group and number them.

■ Jot down the order in which you would write up the lettered groups.

I should organize the information about the 24 hour conference package like this, though your version may well differ from mine.

24 hour conference package	
Full use of conference facilities	B1
Strongly recommended	A1
Accommodation in single rooms with private bathrooms	C2
Coffee and tea are provided during conference	B2
Price includes full English breakfast, lunch and dinner	C1
Available from January 1st	A2
Price is £44 per head	D1
Single rooms have colour television, radio, telephone, tea and coffee making facilities and mini bar	C3
Represents extremely good value for money	D2

And I should write up the lettered groups in the order A; B; C; D.

This section of my letter would probably look something like this:

> May I strongly recommend our special 24 hour conference package which is available from January 1st.
>
> This would enable you to have full use of the conference facilities including tea and coffee whilst the conference is taking place and it also includes full English breakfast, lunch and dinner and overnight accommodation in single rooms. Each single room has a private bathroom, colour television, radio, telephone, tea and coffee making facilities and a mini-bar.
>
> I'm sure you will agree that, at £44 a head, this represents excellent value for money.

A structure plan like the one we have just been using can help us a little further too.

Let's go back for a minute and have another look at part of a letter I wrote from the plan a few pages back.

Here is the extract again.

> Our conference room, the Penshaw Suite, has its own cloakroom and toilets and can be divided into two or three smaller rooms as required.
>
> The whole room measures 54' 6" x 17' 6" x 10'.
>
> But when divided, the two thirds room provides accomodation measuring 36' x 17' 6" x 10' and the one third room provides accommodation measuring 18' x 17' 6" x 10'.
>
> The Penshaw Suite seats 120 people for meetings, a maximum of 100 for buffet service or 80 for lunch or dinner.
>
> We also have 12 syndicate rooms, each seating 12 people and each with its own bathroom.

Although this contains all the information about the conference facilities in a logical order the layout could be improved so that the reader can see at a glance any particular information he is looking for.

Activity 43

■ Time guide 2 minutes

Jot down *two* ways in which you think the layout of this part of the letter could be improved.

_____

_____

_____

_____

I would improve it in the following way – you may have thought of other possibilities as well:

■ use headings and sub-headings for each new topic;

■ number the paragraph and the sub-sections in the paragraph;

■ put the information containing figures together and arrange the figures in vertical columns.

So I feel a better laid out version of the extract would look like this.

1.	**Conference facilities**
1.1	The Penshaw Suite
	Our conference room, the Penshaw Suite, has its own cloakroom and toilets and can be divided into two or three smaller rooms if required.
1.2	Dimensions

Whole room	54' 6" x 17' 6" x 10'
Two thirds room	36' x 17' 6" x 10'
One third room	18' x 17' 6" x 10'

1.3	Seating Capacity
	The Penshaw Suite seats 120 people for meetings, a maximum of 100 for buffet service or 80 for lunch or dinner.
1.4	Syndicate Rooms
	We also have 12 syndicate rooms, each seating 12 people and each with its own bathroom.

3.3
Headings and numbers

Let's look at each of these points separately for a moment.

Using headings
and sub-headings

If you use a structure plan like the one we've already looked at, it is usually fairly obvious what the headings and sub-headings could be.

Using them makes it easier for the reader to identify your plan and helps to transfer the information readily to his mind.

You certainly should use headings and sub-headings in reports and memos, and it's becoming quite usual to do so if you are writing a letter which contains quite a bit of detailed information.

Numbering paragraphs
and sub-sections of
paragraphs

In the same way as headings and sub-headings provide a framework for the reader, so numbered paragraphs and sub-sections help the reader to pick out which points belong together.

It also makes it easy to refer to particular parts of the document if you are discussing it later. It's quicker and easier to say 'In section 3.5 you mention that...' rather than 'When you discuss mechanization you mention that...'. 'Mechanization' could appear anywhere in the document and time is lost while everybody leafs through it to find the right item.

You notice that I've used a decimal numbering system. This is simpler and more consistent than something like 1a, 1b, 2a, 2b, etc., where it's possible, in a fairly lengthy document, to become confused about which letter belongs with which number.

Using a decimal system each number (1.3, 23.4 or whatever) will appear only once, and will relate to only one sub-section.

One point to remember with a decimal system is that it's only the figures *after* the decimal point which change in any one section. So after 1.9, you continue 1.10, 1.11, 1.12 – and don't start to number 1.9, 2.0, 2.1.

Arranging figures in
vertical columns

Because of the way we have been taught to handle figures, we find it easier to compare two or more figures or to relate them to each other if they are shown to us vertically rather than presented in amongst a line of words.

So, if you are writing something which involves several figures, try to arrange them in a simple vertical table.

Activity 44

■ Time guide 10 minutes

On the blank memo form provided rewrite the following memo, improving the layout so that the reader can take in the information more easily.

Memorandum

From: R. Wolley, Unit Manager	To: All Section Leaders
Subject: Telephone Costs	Date: 3 September

I am very concerned about all our rapidly increasing telephone costs. The bill for this quarter is over £1,800 compared with £1,200 this time last year – an increase of over 50 percent.

Bills for the other two quarters this year were approximately £1,400 and £1,500 confirming the upward trend.

We expected that our telephone sales drive would increase costs by 10 percent and there has, of course, also been a 12 percent increase in charges this year. Nevertheless we must do something to reduce the remaining 28 percent increase from this quarter.

Would you please encourage all staff in your section to avoid making calls during the peak rate period 9 a.m.–1 p.m. as much as possible. You might also stress the benefits of preparing for a call before making it so that time spent on the telephone is kept to a minimum. It would also help if staff got into the habit of ringing back or leaving a message rather than holding the line if the person they are calling is not immediately available.

We have never previously attempted to prevent staff making or receiving personal calls – in a small plant like ours there has to be some give and take. I should be grateful, though, if you would ask staff to keep personal calls to a minimum and to use the pay phone in the canteen as far as possible.

R. W.

continued overleaf

Memorandum	
From:	To:
Subject:	Date:

I would lay the memo out like this but, of course, you may have decided to do it slightly differently.

Memorandum	
From: R. Wolley, Unit Manager	To: All Section Leaders
Subject: Telephone Costs	Date: 3 September 1990

1. I am very concerned about our rapidly increasing telephone costs – over 50 percent in the past year as you can see from the figures below.

   Sept. 90   £1,800
   May 90   £1,550
   Jan. 90   £1,400
   Sept. 89   £1,200

2. **Reasons**

   We forecast an increase of 10 percent as a result of our telephone sales drive and there has been a 12 percent increase in telephone charges this year.

3. **Reduction of costs**

   In order to do something about the remaining 28 percent increase from this quarter would you please encourage all staff in your section to:

   3.1 avoid making calls during the peak-rate period 9 a.m.–1 p.m.;

   3.2 prepare for calls before making them to keep time spent on the telephone to a minimum;

   3.3 ring back or leave a message rather than holding on;

   3.4 keep personal calls to a minimum.

4. **Personal Calls**

   We have never previously attempted to prevent staff making or receiving personal calls – in a small plant like ours there has to be some give and take. I should be grateful, though, if you would ask staff to keep personal calls to a minimum and to use the pay phone in the canteen as far as possible.

   R. W.

- Before starting to write, make sure you ask yourself the following

  – Why am I writing this?

  – Who will be reading it?

  – How much do they need to know?

- If achieving your purpose depends on getting a response, try to *encourage* your readers to give it.

- Well-structured writing gets better results:

  – group your material in a logical way;

  – put the groups and items in a logical order;

  – use headings and sub-headings to organize the flow;

  – if there are a lot of headings, give them decimal numbers for easy reference.

CHECKLISTS FOR BUSINESS WRITING

1 Introduction

This part of the unit contains four checklists of points to bear in mind when writing:

● letters;

● memos;

● reports;

● documentation for meetings.

At the beginning of the unit we said that one of the advantages of writing, as opposed to speaking, is that with writing you normally have time to prepare yourself. This is important, because written documents often go on record – and sometimes for a very long time.

It is therefore particularly important to ensure that they are correct.

Very few writers are expert enough to create a perfect document at the first attempt. There will almost always be something in the language, the grammar or the structure which is not quite right.

For that reason it is most important to **draft out** your writing in a rough form **before you commit it to paper**. This advice applies to all kinds of writing, but especially to the types of business writing described in this part of the unit.

Extensions All the extensions mentioned earlier in the unit (and
2-4   listed together on page 92) are all relevant to at least one
             of the kinds of business writing referred to in the next
             few pages.

- If you are answering a letter which contains a reference (such as HS/DT1611-5), make sure you include the reference on your reply.

- Acknowledge the letter you are answering: 'Thank you for your letter of 8 October . . .'.

- If you know the name of the person you are writing to, use it.

- Give your letter a title if that will make the message easier to understand. The title goes *after* Dear Sir, Dear Mr Smith or whatever.

- Use sub-headings and numbered paragraphs if it will help to make the message easier to understand.

- Plan the letter before you write.

  - State briefly what the letter is about:

    'Your North Midlands representative recently suggested that I should contact you about a possible modification to your product line.'

  - Add to your opening statement if necessary:

    'We have successfully adapted your standard product to our requirements and feel that many of your customers could benefit . . .'.

  - State your purpose:

    'If you feel this modification would be of interest, perhaps you would like to come here to see it in operation.'

  - Conclusion:

    'If the dates I suggest are not convenient, perhaps you would telephone me here and we'll arrange a different time.'

- If you begin 'Dear Sir', finish 'Yours faithfully'. If you begin with the person's name ('Dear Mrs Smith'), finish 'Yours sincerely', unless your company has a particular house style which is the same on all letters.

- Never have a post-script (PS). If a letter is so badly thought out that you haven't said all you should in the text of the letter, tear it up and start again.

- Memos ('memo' is short for 'memorandum') are sent instead of letters to people who work in the same company as yourself. You never send a memo to somebody outside the company.

- A memo may be a couple of lines or two pages long but, whatever the length, they all follow the same pattern.

- Many organizations have pre-printed memo pads which are either A4 or A5 size. (A4 is the size this unit is printed on, A5 is half that.) They usually look like this.

Memorandum	
From:	To:
Subject:	Date:

- You fill in the details at the top and this means that you don't have any 'Dear Mr', or 'Dear Mike', or 'Yours sincerely' at the end.

- Memos are usually sent to one other person, but if you need to send one to several people then you make this clear when you fill in the top. Like this, for instance:

Memorandum	
From: Safety Officer	To: All Production Personnel
Subject: Safety Shoes	Date: 3 Dec.

- Like letters and reports, you write memos in complete sentences, not in note form; but you keep it as brief as possible.

- As a general rule you only deal with one subject on one memo. If you have two subjects to discuss or comment on, then you send two memos. This is because the memo will have to be filed under its subject, and you can't easily do that if it deals with several topics.

- A memo shouldn't look like a newspaper article.

  In order to make your memo as simple to understand as possible you should:

  – use sub-headings each time you raise a new point;

  – number each new paragraph.

4   Reports

- Decide the purpose of the report.

  – Is it just to provide information?

  – If so, to whom, and why do they want it?

  – Or are you asked to investigate a problem?

  – If so, precisely what is the problem and how much authority have you to investigate?

- Decide who is going to read the report.

  This will affect how you write it. If it will be read by people in other departments of your company then you will probably have to explain any processes, procedures and technical terms which you use in your own job.

- Check whether there is already a standard form for the report you have to write (e.g. an accident report or dangerous occurrence report form).

- Check whether your company has its own house style for reports. (For example, do they expect recommendations to be at the beginning or the end of the report? Do they expect a separate summary of the report?)

- Collect and organize the material. (Look at page 67 to see one way of doing this.)

- Write the introduction.

  Say what the report is about and why it is necessary. Explain any limiting factors (e.g. shortage of time to investigate further) and any essential background information.

- Under suitable sub-headings, and numbering your paragraphs (look at page 72 for a reminder), describe how you set about collecting the information for the report and what you found out.

- Analyze the information you have given and say what conclusions you draw.

- Write the recommendations. (That is, on the basis of the evidence you have given, what you think should be done.)

  Make recommendations quite specific. A vague recommendation like: 'We should consider trying to reduce waste', is no recommendation at all.

  This is a more meaningful recommendation:

  'It is recommended that we implement the waste reduction programme described from 1 November with the objective of reducing waste by 40 per cent in the following quarter.'

- Don't introduce any new material or arguments into the recommendations. They should be short and very much to the point.

- Write a summary which briefly says what the report is about and what the main recommendations are. Although you have to write this last, it should appear at the beginning of the report so that your readers can quickly get a grasp of what the report contains.

- Check the report for mistakes and to make sure that it still meets your original purpose.

- Sign and date it at the end.

5   Documentation for meetings

**5.1
Notice**

Before a meeting, however informal, let people have written notice of:

- the date;
- the time;
- the place;
- the subject to be discussed.

The agenda is the list of topics to be discussed. It should be clearly defined well before the meeting.

Here is an example of a formal agenda. Even if you don't need such a formal document, there are several points worth copying.

Agenda

1. Apologies for absence   ←   look around at the beginning. Note who's there *and* who's missing. They'll need to be kept informed

2. Minutes of the previous meeting   ←   this means that you read out and agree the written record of what happened at the last meeting

3. Correspondence

4. Cost saving programme – report

5. New warehouse – revision of schedule

6. Issue of protective clothing to warehouse personnel

7. Any other business   ←   this gives people an opportunity to discuss matters which have arisen too late to be included on the agenda. It's up to the Chairman to decide how much discussion to allow

8. Date, time and place of next meeting   ←   If you need to have another meeting, fix the details *now*. If not the group easily runs out of steam. The time between meetings becomes longer and the group loses interest and effectiveness.

This is the written record of what took place at the meeting.

● Write notes for the minutes *during* the meeting. (Or, if you are chairing the discussion, ask somebody to do it for you.)

● Write up the minutes within 24 hours of the meeting, otherwise you forget what was said.

Here is an extract from some minutes, which shows you how they should be set out.

Northern Fashionscene Ltd

Minutes of the meeting of the Works Committee held at 9.30 a.m. on Monday 3 December 1990

Those present: J. Harman (Chairman)
                    M. Ashford
                    E. Jackson
                    D. Davies
                    L. Simpson
                    J. Easby

1. Apologies were received from A. Whitehead.

2. The minutes of the Works Committee held on Monday 5 November 1990 were read and approved.

3. *Matters arising*

   M. Ashford, Personnel Manager, said that following the last meeting, he had investigated complaints from personnel concerning local bus services and was able to report.

4. *Personnel Manager's report*

   4.1 Following complaints by personnel that they arrived late and had to leave early because of cut-backs in bus services, the United Bus Company had been approached. They confirmed that there was:

       a withdrawal of duplicate buses at peak periods;

       a cut-back in services at peak-load times.

       United Bus Company regretted the situation but felt that they could not offer any improvement in the near future.

   4.2 Records of staff turnover for the past three years showed a gradually increasing staff turnover rate (3 per cent – 7 per cent).

Here is an example of Action Minutes, which are the form of minute you're likely to find most useful at work. As you see, they mainly record the action to be taken and, in the right hand column, give the initials of the people responsible for taking action.

These are simple and quick to write up and to read and are an effective way of pointing out to people exactly what you want *them* to do before the next meeting.

A. Bryson Engineering

Minutes of the meeting of the Health and Safety Committee held at the Stockbridge plant on 25 February 1990.

Those present: B. Williams – Plant Engineer,
                  C. Gaffey – Safety Officer,
                  S. O'Toole – Medical Officer,
                  H. Higgins, S. Clarke and A. Peters – Health and Safety Representatives.

Minutes	Action to be taken by
The emission of fumes from C plant has been totally controlled for the past quarter. B. Williams agreed to install a permanent monitoring device to ensure that control continues.	B. W.
C. Gaffey reported that new lightweight protective overalls suitable for production areas were now available. Messrs Higgins, Clarke and Peters agreed to organize distribution in A, B and C plants.	H.H., S.C., A.P.
The committee agreed that the plant needs a permanent full-time nurse rather than the present part-time arrangement. S. O'Toole agreed to draft a report for the next meeting on the nursing provision made in other engineering companies of a similar size in the area.	S. O'T

1   Quick quiz

Well done – you have completed the unit. Now listen to the questions on Side one of the audio cassette. If you are not sure about some of the answers, check back in the workbook before making up your mind.

Write down your answers in the space below.

1 _____

_____

2 _____

_____

3 _____

_____

4 _____

_____

5 _____

_____

6 _____

_____

7 _____

_____

8 _____

_____

9 _____

_____

10 _____

_____

11 _____

_____

12 _____

_____

13 _____

_____

14 _____

_____

15 _____

_____

2   Action check

On Side two of the audio cassette, you will hear a number of people speaking in various situations.

Listen carefully to each extract.

Write your answers and comments in the space below.

Situation 1: taking notes _____

_____

_____

_____

_____

_____

Situation 2: giving notes _____

_____

_____

_____

_____

_____

Situation 3: cutting out the waffle

Anyone who knew anything at all about people management could be forgiven for arriving at the conclusion that the reason why the supervisor in question failed to engineer a more appropriate outcome was that she was lacking in the basic skills which one would normally expect to find in a person occupying such a responsible position.

In my own personal opinion such a conclusion would indeed be justified and no-one should be surprised if this impacts on that person's future career.

New version: _____

_____

_____

_____

_____

_____

_____

_____

Situation 4: backing up **List the key points here:**
the briefing

_____

_____

_____

_____

_____

_____

_____

_____

_____

_____

3   Unit assessment

Time guide 60 minutes

Case
Study

Read the following two letters and then deal with the task which follows, writing your answer on a separate sheet of paper.

The first letter is from a prospective customer, the owner of a hotel in Yorkshire who wants to plant the grounds of the hotel with roses and who is asking for details of what rose trees are available.

The second is from the Customer Service supervisor of A. Savage & Son, specialist rose growers. As you see, the letter from A. Savage & Son contains some useful information but it isn't very well expressed, or logically arranged, or well presented, so that the customer can quickly grasp what he is being told.

Rewrite the letter from A Savage & Son, using the same information to answer the customer's enquiry but expressing it more simply, logically and helpfully.

You will need to think about:

● the words and phrases used;

● the style;

● the grouping of the main points included;

● the overall structure.

HAWKGARTH HOTEL
Exelby, North Yorkshire

A. Savage & Son   4 August 1990
Reading Road
Binchester
Berkshire
BC2 6QX

Dear Sir

I read with interest the article 'Roses for all reasons' in the Sunday Mail yesterday in which you were mentioned as providing a free advisory service on planting and cultivating roses.

This hotel stands in two acres of grounds which used to be well known in the area for its splendid display of roses. We have several interesting photographs taken before the Second World War which bear this out. However, its requisition during the war as a military establishment, subsequent years of neglect followed by fifteen years use as boarding school means that the former rose gardens have virtually disappeared.

I anticipate that re-stocking the grounds will take about five years and thought in terms of starting this year with hedges, roses amongst the trees in the woodland and climbers in difficult positions which will all take some years to achieve maturity.

I should be interested to know therefore what you would suggest for the following:

1. Climbers for a north facing, random stone wall of the main wing of the hotel, approximately 80 feet long;

2. A vigorous tall hedge to screen adjoining farm buildings and to deter animals from the farm from coming through the fence onto our property;

3. Ramblers to grow amongst trees on the edge of an existing copse of trees (rather neglected at the moment) in a shaded corner of the grounds. I hoped that planting some roses there would give colour and interest to an otherwise rather dull area.

I look forward to hearing from you.

Yours faithfully

S. Hamlin

A. Savage & Son
Rose Specialist
Reading Road
BINCHESTER
Berkshire
BC2 6QX

Mr S. Hamlin   7 August 1990
Hawkgarth Hotel
EXELBY
North Yorkshire

Dear Sir

With reference to your letter of 4 August, we shall be delighted to help you re-stock your rose garden and offer the following suggestions. A copy of our catalogue is enclosed so that you can consider the entire stock list for yourself. The ideal planting time for roses is November/December, though any time until March is possible provided there is no danger of severe frost. However, I do advise you to place your order as soon as possible so that the roses are despatched in time for autumn planting provided, of course, that you are ready to plant them then. Our roses are packed in peat and polythene and will tolerate being kept in dark, frost-free conditions for up to three weeks prior to planting.

As I said, you may like to choose alternatives from the complete stock list but I suggest the following. Alberic Barbier would do well climbing against a north wall and will also grow into trees satisfactorily, though you would have to be careful that roses were not planted too close to the roots of trees and, of course, no roses will do well in totally shaded conditions. However, I think you would find that the following would achieve the effect you want in adding interest and colour to the copse:

Alberic Barbier;
Dr van Fleet;
Bobbie James;
Pauls Himalayan Must;
Wedding Day.

This would give you a variety of colour and flowering periods and the additional interest of coloured hips in the autumn.

In addition to Alberic Barbier as a climber for a north wall, you might like to try Gloire de Dijon, Golden Showers, May Queen and New Dawn. This will also give you a variety of colour. You are fortunate in having random stone walls against which almost every colour is seen to advantage as opposed to brick, for instance, which never does justice to reds and crimsons. However, against a north facing wall, with limited direct sunlight, I think you will find that lighter yellows, pinks and whites create a more pleasing effect. Incidentally, May Queen also makes a splendid tree. As for the hedge, I Suggest Nevada, Constance Spry and Fruhlings Gold to give you a variety of colour, though, of course, if you feel that one colour would create a more dramatic effect then you could create a hedge of any one of these. Certainly any of them will give you a tall, impenetrable hedge within a few years.

Judging by the indication of size you have given, I estimate that you would need twelve climbers and fifteen to twenty roses to grow into the copse. You don't give an indication of the length of hedge you require but, to provide a dense hedge of this type you could estimate planting one bush every four feet.

Climbers and the roses for the copse are £3.75 each, hedging plants are £2.75 and we give a discount of 10 percent on orders over £200. There is a standard charge of £4 per order for packaging and carriage but this is waived on orders over £50.

We can offer a more detailed advisory service than I have given if you provide more detailed information of dimensions, aspect, soil type etc and, if required, we will also come and visit a customer's premises to discuss special requirements though we have to charge for this service. I enclose a questionnare which you might like to complete and return if you would like more detailed advice on planting your grounds. This service is free.

I wish you every success with your roses and we look forward to receiving your order.

Yours faithfully

R. Harris
Customer Service Supervisor

Enc

Time guide 60 minutes

The time guide for this assignment gives you an approximate idea of how long it is likely to take you to write up your findings.

You will need to spend some additional time gathering information, perhaps talking to colleagues and thinking about the assignment. The result of your efforts should be presented on separate sheets of paper.

Choose what seems to you a fairly limited problem at work to which you can think of a solution. This might be:

- a minor change in a clerical system;

- a slightly different way of working;

- a change of material or materials handling;

- a change of storage arrangements;

- something to do with the health, safety or welfare of your workteam

But those are only suggestions. You may well think of something which doesn't come in any of these categories, and exactly what you choose will depend on the nature of your job.

Perhaps you will think of a problem which you have solved fairly recently. In that case, use it for this project, but assume that your solution hasn't yet been put into operation.

Don't choose anything too ambitious because, as you know, it's rarely simple to bring about a major change in one work area without affecting the work of a lot of other people.

Having chosen your problem and its solutions, write a memo to your immediate boss describing precisely what the problem is and what you suggest to improve the situation. Remember to provide enough evidence to support your case and write it in a way which is likely to get a favourable response.

Next assume that what you propose has been agreed to and you can make the change.

How would you inform your workteam?

Would you need to back up anything you say in writing? In one or two sentences write down what you would do to make sure that your workteam took notice of the change you were making and remembered it whenever necessary.

Finally, write out *one* of the pieces of written information which you might use to get your workteam to make the change you suggest effectively and efficiently. This might be a memo, a notice or notes for a briefing session, but need not necessarily be any of these.

Return to objectives

Having completed your work on this unit, let us review each of our unit opening objectives.

You will be *better able to*:

● identify when and why you need to write;

There's nothing particularly special about putting things in writing. Speaking and writing can both be equally effective means of communicating with other people and either can be just what is needed in certain circumstances. You wouldn't, for instance, just tell somebody details of a pay rise without giving them some written confirmation of it and you wouldn't ask one of your workteam who seemed depressed and unable to work properly to jot his worries down on a piece of paper. So there's nothing especially superior about writing. It's just that it does have the advantage of allowing people to refer to it later, if they have to remember details of something slightly complicated, or something which is likely to be open to argument or discussion. And, of course, if you are planning something which hasn't yet happened, like a meeting, then details in writing allow other people to plan too, and thus you make more effective use of your own time and theirs.

So if you now feel that writing things down is not just something which you have to do in certain limited circumstances, but is a communication tool which you can use, judging each situation on its merits, whenever you feel that written information will help people remember, or prepare, better than the spoken word alone would do, then you have achieved this objective.

● make your style of writing simple, direct and appropriate for the reader and the task;

The days when business writing was expected to sound rather long-winded and full of jargon phrases like 'I am in receipt of yours of the 3rd inst.' are fortunately over. But it's still a very natural temptation to write in a rather more wordy style than we would use if we were talking to the same person. Yet everybody appreciates a simple, clear (and preferably short) letter, memo, report or whatever it is that we are faced with reading. Writing simply isn't necessarily easy, it involves thinking for yourself rather than using over-worked expressions which other people have used, and deliberately pausing to ask yourself if one word will do instead of three. It isn't something that you become skilled in overnight, not at the end of working through a unit on the subject for that matter! But if you have found the practical hints in this unit of some use and, when you pick up your pen, you now ask yourself 'Now how would *I* say this', rather than letting the words form themselves, then you have probably achieved this objective.

● organize your writing so that your ideas and messages are easy to understand;

Simple, clear writing alone isn't always enough to make sure that what you write is readily understood and acted upon.

When we're faced with a page of written information we usually read it at least twice, unless it's very simple – once to get the general drift of what it's about and once to read it in detail.

If you can signpost what your writing is about by appropriate headings, sub-headings and numbered paragraphs which are in a logical order, you speed up and reinforce the reader's understandi And, since most people who are working are pretty busy, your rea will appreciate your clarity and be more likely to respond.

● ensure your writing achieves results.

You improve your chances of getting the response you want if you let the reader know what you want him to do – whether it's to supply some information, come to a meeting, contact you, or whatever.

If you do both these it means you have thought about the purpose of what you're writing and the surest way of achieving it. This may only take a matter of seconds or, if it is quite a lengthy report or letter you are writing, may be the hardest part of the whole task. Either way, if you now find that, before you write something, you pause to consider why you're writing and how to organize it to achieve what you want, then you have achieved this objective.

I hope that the work you have done was enjoyable and useful enoug to encourage you to continue your studies.

2	Extensions

Extension 1

Many people have difficulty with plurals, and end up getting them wrong. A common mistake is to use an apostrophe-S, as in these examples:

'Lettuce's only 40p.'

'Girl's and boy's wanted for delivering newspaper's.'

For most words, the correct way to form a plural is simply to add S:

Singular	Plural
ratchet	ratchets
programme	programmes
warehouse	warehouses
inspector	inspectors
kitten	kittens
colleague	colleagues
tree	trees
breakfast	breakfasts
album	albums
limb	limbs
pudding	puddings
expedition	expeditions

Never use apostrophe-S to make a plural: ***limb's*** and ***programme's*** are wrong.

With some words, you make the plural by adding ES:

Singular	Plural
watch	watches
carcass	carcasses
tomato	tomatoes

Words which end in Y, change to IES:

Singular	Plural
city	cities
activity	activities

And there are some very common words which change in different ways:

Singular	Plural
woman	women
mouse	mice
sheaf	sheaves
goose	geese

So when do we use the apostrophe-S?

It **never** indicates a plural. **Either** it is a shortened version of 'is' or 'has', **or** it indicates belonging.

Short for is or has	Belonging
The ratchet's broken.	The ratchet's teeth are broken.
The summons's on the table.	The summons's wording is wrong.
The city's a mess.	So are the city's inhabitants.

The word that writers most often get wrong is **its/it's**.

Its without an apostrophe indicates 'belonging to'; **it's** with an apostrophe is short for **it is** or **it has**. For example:

'Look at that mouse – it's lost its tail!'

Correct spelling means learning words as you go along. No-one can claim to spell everything perfectly, because there are so many long and complicated words in the language. But it is very embarrassing to have your spelling corrected, and it is well worth trying to improve your spelling skills.

Extension 2

Book: *The Complete Plain Words*

Author: E. Gowers

Publisher: Pelican paperbacks, London

Although it was written quite a long time ago, in 1948, this book is still one of the best guides to how to make your writing more livel, readable and clear. Chapters 5, 6, 7 and 8 are about how to choose words which are straightforward, familiar and clear in their meaning.

Extension 3

Book: *The Janner Letterwriter*

Author: G. Janner, MP

Publisher: Business Books, Century Hutchinson, London

Mr Janner is a well-known expert on business communications, and in this book he provides guidance on how to write clear and grammatical letters in every possible business context. It includes sample openings and closes, as well as numerous other practical hints.

Extension 4

Book: *Mastering Business Communications*

Authors: L. A. Woolcott and W. R. Unwin

Publisher: Macmillan, London

This book contains several useful chapters dealing with writing reports as well as other routine kinds of business communications: letters, memos, notices and minutes.

In addition to these Extensions, you may be interested to watch a series of videos produced by The Open College entitled *In Charge*. These illustrate a number of aspects of supervisory work.

These Extensions and the videos can be taken up via your Support Centre. They will arrange for you to have access to them. However, it may be more convenient to check out the materials with your personnel or training people at work – they could well give you access. There are good reasons for approaching your own people as, by doing so, they will become aware of your continuing interest in the subject and you will be able to involve them in your development.